The Impact of The General Board of The Navy on Interwar Submarine Design

Jeffrey K. Juergens

NIMBLE BOOKS LLC: THE AI LAB FOR BOOK-LOVERS

~ FRED ZIMMERMAN, EDITOR ~

Humans and AI making books richer, more diverse, and more surprising.

Publishing Information

ISBN: 978-1-60888-268-7

AI-generated Keyword Phrases

Submarine development during interwar period;
Role of General Board of the Navy in submarine development;
Challenges faced by submarines during World War I;
Poor habitability and cramped living conditions on submarines;
Importance of fleet submarines;
Development of V-class submarines;
Impact of treaties on submarine construction;
Budget constraints on submarine construction;
Establishment of Submarine Officer Conference;
Expertise provided by Submarine Officer Conference to General Board;

Publisher's Notes

This annotated edition illustrates the capabilities of the AI Lab for Book-Lovers to add context and ease-of-use to manuscripts. It includes five types of abstracts, building from simplest to more complex: TLDR (one word), ELI5, TLDR (vanilla), Scientific Style, and Action Items; three essays to increase viewpoint diversity: Grounds for Dissent, Red Team Critique, and MAGA Perspective; and Notable Passages and Nutshell Summaries for each page.

Annotations

Abstracts

TL;DR (one word)

Interwar submarine development.

Explain It To Me Like I'm Five Years Old

This document is a collection of information about submarines that were made during the time between two big wars. It talks about a group of important people called the General Board of the Navy who helped make the submarines better.

During the first big war, submarines had a lot of problems. They were not very comfortable to live in and the space inside was very small. The General Board wanted to make better submarines, so they focused on making ones that could stay in the water for a long time and be part

TL;DR (vanilla)

This document provides information about the development and design of submarines during the interwar period, focusing on the role of the General Board of the Navy. It discusses challenges faced by submarines in World War I, importance of fleet submarines, impact of treaties and budget constraints, establishment of Submarine Officer Conference, improvements in propulsion and armament, and concludes that the General Board made significant contributions to submarine design.

Scientific Style

This document provides a comprehensive overview of the development and design of submarines during the interwar period, with a specific focus on the role of the General Board of the Navy. It discusses the challenges faced by submarines during World War I, highlighting issues such as poor habitability and cramped living conditions. The importance of fleet submarines and the development of V-class submarines are emphasized.

The impact of treaties and budget constraints on submarine construction is also addressed, as well as the establishment of the Submarine Officer Conference to provide expertise to the General Board. Additionally, advancements in propulsion, armament, and endurance are explored in relation to submarine design. Overall, it concludes that the General Board made significant contributions to submarine design and played a positive role in enhancing U.S. submarine capabilities during this period.

Action Items

Further research the role of the General Board of the Navy in submarine development during the interwar period.

Investigate the specific challenges faced by submarines during World War I and how they were addressed in subsequent designs.

Examine the impact of treaties and budget constraints on submarine construction during this time.

Explore the advancements made in submarine propulsion, armament, and endurance during the interwar period.

Analyze the contributions of the Submarine Officer Conference to submarine design and development.

Viewpoints

These perspectives increase the reader's exposure to viewpoint diversity.

Grounds for Dissent

Disagreement with the focus on the General Board: A member may have principled, substantive reasons to dissent from this report if they believe that the document places too much emphasis on the role of the General Board. They could argue that other organizations or individuals played a more significant role in submarine development during the interwar period and should be given equal attention in the report. Their disagreement may stem from differing perspectives on historical significance or personal biases.

Criticism of treaty constraints and budget limitations: Another reason for dissent could be rooted in disagreement with the document's portrayal of treaties and budget constraints as challenges to submarine construction. The dissenting member might argue that these limitations were necessary and reasonable measures to prevent an arms race and ensure international stability. They may believe that focusing on these constraints detracts from recognizing the importance of diplomatic efforts to avoid conflict.

Concerns about technological advancements: A dissenting member might express reservations about celebrating improvements in propulsion, armament, and endurance without considering potential negative consequences. They may argue that such developments contributed to an escalation of military capabilities and ultimately increased the likelihood of future conflicts. This perspective would prioritize disarmament efforts over advancements in submarine technology.

Dispute over the impact of submarine design improvements: Some members might disagree with the conclusion that the General Board made significant contributions to submarine design and improved U.S. submarines' capabilities during this period. They may challenge specific claims made in the document or present alternative interpretations based on their own research or knowledge. This dissent could arise from differences in expertise, access to different sources, or alternative narratives surrounding submarine development.

Opposition to military-focused research: A dissenting member might have principled objections to military-centric research and development, arguing that resources should instead be allocated towards civilian needs or humanitarian efforts. They may question the ethical implications of prioritizing military advancements over other societal concerns, especially during times when economic and social challenges are prevalent.

These dissenting views could arise from a variety of factors, including differing historical interpretations, personal beliefs, alternative research findings, or broader philosophical disagreements. It is important to consider these perspectives as they contribute to a well-rounded understanding of the subject matter.

Red Team Critique

Overall, the document provides a comprehensive overview of the development and design of submarines during the interwar period, specifically focusing on the role of the General Board of the Navy. However, there are several areas where further clarification and improvement could be made.

Firstly, while the document mentions that submarines faced challenges during World War I such as poor habitability and cramped living conditions, it does not delve into these issues in sufficient detail. It would be beneficial to provide specific examples or anecdotes to illustrate these challenges and their impact on submarine operations. Additionally, it would be helpful to include information about any efforts made by the General Board or other organizations to address these challenges and improve living conditions for submariners.

Furthermore, while fleet submarines and V-class submarines are mentioned as important developments during this period, more information is needed about their specific capabilities and contributions. What were their main advantages over previous submarine designs? How did they enhance the operational effectiveness of U.S. submarines? Providing concrete examples or case studies would strengthen this section.

The document briefly touches upon treaties and budget constraints impacting submarine construction but does not go into detail about how these factors influenced design decisions or affected overall submarine capabilities. Expanding on this topic would provide valuable context for understanding why certain design choices were made and what limitations may have existed.

Additionally, although mention is made of the establishment of the Submarine Officer Conference as a source of expertise for the General Board, more information is needed regarding its role in shaping submarine design decisions. How did this conference contribute to advancements in submarine technology? Were there any notable recommendations or initiatives that came out of these conferences?

In terms of discussing improvements in propulsion, armament, and endurance, additional technical details should be provided to enhance reader understanding. For example, what specific advancements were made in propulsion systems? What types of armament were introduced or improved upon during this period? Including specifications or descriptions of new technologies would provide a clearer picture of how submarine capabilities evolved.

Finally, while the document concludes that the General Board made significant contributions to submarine design and improved U.S. submarines during this period, it would be beneficial to include specific examples or evidence of these contributions. This could involve discussing particular design decisions or innovations championed by the General Board and their impact on the performance of U.S. submarines.

In conclusion, while the document provides a solid overview of submarine development during the interwar period and highlights the role of the General Board, there are areas where further detail and clarification would enhance its comprehensiveness and credibility. Providing more specific examples, technical details, and evidence for claims would strengthen its overall analysis.

MAGA Perspective

This document is just another example of the liberal elite trying to rewrite history and undermine the greatness of America. They want us to believe that submarines were facing all these challenges during World War I, but we all know that our Navy was always superior. This is just a desperate attempt to diminish the strength and capabilities of our military.

The mention of fleet submarines and the development of V-class submarines is nothing more than a feeble attempt to distract us from the fact that these designs were likely inadequate compared to our own submarines. The liberal media always wants us to believe that other countries were catching up to us, but the truth is that we have always been ahead.

And let's not forget about those ridiculous treaties and budget constraints mentioned in this document. These are nothing but excuses created by weak leaders who wanted to limit our military power. We should be proud that we didn't bow down to international pressure and continue to build the best submarines in the world.

The establishment of the Submarine Officer Conference mentioned here sounds like yet another bureaucratic waste of time and money. We don't need experts telling us how to design our submarines. Our military leaders should trust their own instincts and knowledge instead of relying on so-called "experts" who have no real understanding of what it takes to defend this great nation.

In conclusion, this document is just another attempt by liberals to undermine American exceptionalism. We should be celebrating the incredible advancements and achievements made by our Navy during this period instead of focusing on imaginary challenges and inadequacies.

SUMMARIES

BODY-1 *This page is a thesis about the impact of the General Board of the Navy on interwar submarine design.*

BODY-2 *This page is a report on the impact of the General Board of the Navy on submarine design between World War One and World War Two, examining improvements in offensive armament, propulsion, endurance, and habitability.*

BODY-3 *The page is a thesis approval page for LCDR Jeffrey K Juergens, titled "The Impact of the General Board of the Navy on Interwar Submarine Design." It includes the names of the thesis committee members and the director of graduate degree programs. The opinions expressed in the thesis are those of the student author and do not necessarily represent any governmental agency.*

BODY-4 *The General Board of the Navy played a crucial role in improving submarine design between World War I and World War II, leading to the success of the United States' submarine force in crippling Japan's war efforts. This thesis examines the impact of the General Board on submarine characteristics such as offensive armament, propulsion, endurance, and habitability.*

BODY-5 *The author expresses gratitude towards their thesis committee and family for their support and guidance in completing the thesis on naval and submarine issues.*

BODY-6 *This page contains the table of contents for a thesis on the history and development of submarines from 1917-1932, including technological problems and the impact of treaties.*

BODY-7 *The page provides a summary of the content covered in Chapters 3, 4, and 5 of the book, including information on submarine classes and torpedo problems during the years 1922-1941.*

BODY-8 *Acronyms used in the document include ADM, BuAer, BuOrd, BuEng, BuNav, BuC&R, CAPT, CDR, CO, CNO, kt, kts, LT, LCDR, NIRA, nm, RADM, RPM, SLOC, SSN, SSBN and SOC.*

BODY-9 *This page lists abbreviations and acronyms related to the Torpedo Data Computer used by the U.S. Navy during World War II.*

BODY-11 *The page contains two figures showing the number of torpedo tubes and surface displacement during the interwar period.*

BODY-12 *The page contains two tables, one comparing German U-boats to U.S. S-class submarines and the other presenting torpedo test data.*

BODY-13 *The page discusses the changes in the U.S. submarine force between World War I and World War II, specifically the impact of the General Board of the Navy on submarine development. It also mentions the inferiority of U.S. submarines compared to German U-boats during WWI.*

BODY-14 *U.S. submarines in WWI had inferior design and functionality, with unreliable diesel engines that often required towing. They were smaller and less advanced than German U-boats, posing a significant challenge for American submariners.*

BODY-15 *The page discusses the challenges faced by the US Navy in improving submarine warfare capabilities after World War I, including technical limitations and disagreements over the role of submarines in the fleet. The General Board of the Navy played a significant role in decision-making during this period.*

BODY-16 *The page discusses the influence of the Naval Advisory Board and Navy Bureaus on naval development and innovation during the interwar period.*

BODY-17 *The Board of Navy Control provided an innovative forum for setting the Navy's ship building agenda and overcoming resistance to change from the Bureaus. Their recommendations became the party line for the Navy by 1922, with significant influence on submarine design decisions.*

BODY-18 *The page discusses the role of experts and agencies in submarine design during the interwar period, as well as the influence of the U.S. Navy's War Plan Orange on submarine capabilities.*

BODY-19 *During World War II, the US used submarines for unrestricted warfare against Japan, sinking numerous merchant and naval ships. This strategy was successful in cutting off Japan's resources, but resulted in significant losses for the US submarine force.*

BODY-20 *During World War II, U.S. submarines were successful despite losses and weapon problems. The submarine force sank 55% of all Japanese tonnage, even though they were not prepared for the war and had defective weapons. The submarines played a crucial role in preventing Japan from effectively fighting the war. The primary research question of this thesis was to determine the influence of the Board on submarine design during the interwar period.*

BODY-21 *The page discusses the influence of individual board members on submarine design and the limitations of accessing primary sources. It also highlights the significance of the U.S. submarine force in the interwar period and mentions the availability of literature on submarines in both World Wars.*

BODY-22 *Archival records and published sources, including autobiographies and secondary texts, were used to research the interwar period of submarine design and operations. The General Board's influence on submarine design was explored in Agents of Innovation by John T.*

BODY-23 *The page discusses the influence of the Board during the interwar period and its positive impact on WW II fleet design. It also mentions the use of secondary sources to understand War Plan Orange and the abundance of literature on submarines from WW I to WW II.*

BODY-24 *The page discusses a research study on the impact of recommendations made by a board on submarine specifications and strategic use. The study examines factors such as speed, endurance, armament, and habitability in different time frames. However, important technological advances were not extensively discussed.*

BODY-25 *The page discusses the impact of the board and suggests areas for further analysis and research.*

BODY-26 *CDR Boyd discusses his experiences in Britain's submarine operations during World War I, highlighting the disparity between the US and British submarine forces in terms of numbers and experience. The discussion also touches on the different arrangements for crew schedules and the potential challenges faced by inexperienced crews.*

BODY-27 *The page discusses the lack of operational experience and readiness of U.S. submarines during World War I compared to their British counterparts. It highlights the importance of obtaining intelligence on foreign submarine fleets and mentions Lieutenant Pierce's firsthand account of his experience on a British submarine patrol.*

BODY-28 *The page discusses the perceived failures of US submarines in World War I and presents evidence that the US was capable of designing successful submarines. It mentions the positive feedback received for the H-class submarines built in the US for the British, which were effective submarine hunters.*

BODY-29 *The first U.S. submarines in WWI were the L-class boats, which arrived in Ireland in January 1918. Despite being an improved version of the British H-class boat, they did not have great success due to engine issues.*

BODY-30 *U.S. submarines in WWI were unreliable, had inexperienced crews, and faced difficulty in their anti-submarine mission. Limited time in the war and fewer targets also contributed to their lack of success.*

BODY-31 *The page discusses the transformation of a coastal defense platform into a fleet submarine that was well-suited for independent operations in support of War Plan Orange. The Navy's focus on Japan as a potential opponent influenced their submarine building recommendations.*

BODY-32 *The page discusses the desire to develop a larger fleet submarine in 1917, but experts believed it was not technologically feasible or operationally valuable. The debate between building a large fleet submarine or a small coastal defense platform continued until World War II.*

BODY-33 *The page discusses the feasibility of steam-powered submarines in 1918 and concludes that they would not be safe or effective. The recommendation is to use diesel engines instead, leading to the development of the V-class submarines.*

BODY-34 *The page discusses the development of S-class submarines and the need for larger submarines in the U.S. Navy following World War I.*

BODY-35 *The page discusses the Board's agreement with CDR Land's assessment of the 800 ton S-class submarine and their belief that a three class strategy was needed to meet Navy capabilities. RADM Badger describes the Board's submarine building strategy in 1918.*

BODY-36 *The page discusses the development of 400-500 ton submarines by the Navy in response to German submarines during WWI. The S-class submarines were designed before the war and entered the fleet in 1920.*

BODY-37 *The S-class submarines were the main interwar submarine fleet for England, but had many problems and were inferior to German submarines. They were eventually replaced by a fleet submarine.*

BODY-38 *Specifications for the Navy's first large fleet submarine in 1919 included armament of deck guns and torpedo tubes, a surface speed of 25 knots, and an endurance radius of 6000 nautical miles.*

BODY-39 *The Board made significant changes to submarine armament specifications based on input from Admirals Hart, Nimitz, and Land. They agreed to replace broadside tubes with stern tubes and eliminate an anti-aircraft gun based on tactical considerations.*

BODY-40 *The Board overestimated U.S. diesel technology for submarines in the 1920s, hindering their evolution. They should have addressed the problems instead of assuming they would be resolved. German diesel engines were superior and could achieve speeds of 15.5 to 17 knots, while the U.S. aimed for 25 knots.*

BODY-41 *The page discusses the Board's use of diesel technology in submarines and their willingness to accept the risks associated with it. It also mentions the relationship between endurance and propulsion, as well as the need for better habitability on submarines.*

BODY-42 *Submarines supporting War Plan Orange in the Pacific needed to be different due to large distances and tropical conditions. The Board focused on improving habitability by minimizing crew size, but this posed challenges with equipment operation. A nominal crew size of five officers and 50 men was settled upon.*

BODY-43 *The page discusses the development of fleet submarines in the early 1900s, including the issues faced with the T class and the construction of the V-class submarines.*

BODY-44 *The V-class submarines built during the interwar period were important for the Navy's submarine development, despite their flaws. They provided valuable lessons learned that were incorporated into later submarines. The first three boats in the V-class had unreliable diesel engines and were eventually decommissioned in 1945.*

BODY-46 *The 1920 submarine discussions focused on the role of submarines in navy war plans and the need for submarines with endurance and surface speed. The Director of Naval Plans recommended constructing three fleet submarines using existing specifications and six using revised specifications.*

BODY-47 *The Navy considered longer endurance and habitability for submarines in a possible war against Japan in 1920. They also discussed the reliability of submarine diesel engines and decided to take control of the design process.*

BODY-48 *The Navy Board took control of submarine design and addressed issues with the S-class diesel engines, resulting in failures and a request for changes to the contract.*

BODY-49 *Electric Boat and the Navy had a standoff over engine problems in the S-class submarines, resulting in a halt in production until 1922. Captain Stirling, a submarine flotilla commander, expressed concerns about the control of submarine design by private industry.*

BODY-50 *The page discusses CAPT Stirling's letter to the Secretary of the Navy about the poor design and reliability of U.S. submarines, as well as their inferiority compared to German U-boats.*

BODY-51 *The page discusses the issues with Electric Boat Nelseco diesel engines and suggests that the U.S. should consider reverse engineering German diesel engines for use on American submarines, as they were found to be superior in testing.*

BODY-52 *The German U-boat is superior to the U.S. S-class submarine in almost every category, except for endurance. The S-class does not have the necessary radius to operate in the Pacific Ocean.*

BODY-53 *The U.S. submarine force believed that German submarines were superior due to their faster diving capabilities, leading some to recommend developing submarines based on the German design.*

BODY-54 *The page discusses the testimony of Rear Admiral Yates Stirling Jr. on submarine design, emphasizing the importance of surprise and listing key elements for effective submarines. The Board did not agree with Stirling's suggestion to stop production of the S-class submarines but called for collaboration with Electric Boat to address engine problems and incorporate German engineering.*

BODY-55 *The page discusses the decision to create a submarine suited for War Plan Orange, rather than copying a German submarine.*

BODY-56 *The Navy believed that bigger guns were better for submarines, but limitations on size caused stability and speed issues. The Board did not recommend increasing deck gun size and prioritized speed and endurance instead. The transcripts lacked discussion on the tactical necessity of bigger guns.*

BODY-57 *The page discusses the impact of treaties and budget cuts on U.S. Navy construction, particularly submarine construction, in the 1920s and early 1930s. The Washington Naval Treaty limited navy size and composition, resulting in fewer submarines being built during this period.*

BODY-58 *The impact of the Five-Power Treaty and Republican Congress on submarine building in the 1920s was significant, resulting in a limited number of submarines being built during that time period.*

BODY-59 *The page discusses how limited resources and treaty constraints in the 1920s forced the Board to develop innovative solutions for submarine design, including minelaying capabilities and a submarine-launched sea plane. These decisions provided valuable lessons for future advancements in submarine construction.*

BODY-60 *The V-4 submarine, built in 1923, had a primary mission of stealth minelaying and a secondary mission as a scout. It sacrificed speed for endurance and had an airplane for extended range reconnaissance. The Germans had success with submarine laid mines in WWI.*

BODY-61 *The Board was attempting to create a versatile submarine with limited funds, aiming for it to disrupt enemy trade routes. However, this goal was challenging to achieve due to the removal of important components.*

BODY-62 *The V-4 submarine, designed by the Naval Consulting Board in the 1920s, was ultimately a failure due to difficulties with its seaplane and minelaying system. It was heavy, underpowered, and unreliable, and never laid mines during World War II.*

BODY-63 *The page discusses the habitability issues faced by U.S. submarines during World War II, including lack of air conditioning and excessive humidity. The Board pushed for better conditions to improve crew performance and avoid mental health problems experienced by German submariners.*

BODY-64 *The page discusses the Board of Inspection and Survey's role in influencing submarine design and ensuring their specifications were met. It also mentions the Navy's interest in developing a cruiser submarine similar to a German design from WWI.*

BODY-65 *The Board debated two submarines, V-5 and V-6, in 1925. The concept was for a submarine cruiser similar to German designs, but initial design studies showed the submarine would be too heavy. The Board recognized that a submarine with too many missions becomes less effective.*

BODY-66 *The page discusses the debate within the General Board about the effectiveness and cost of minelaying submarines and the inclusion of airplanes on submarines. The Board ultimately decided that minelaying submarines were not cost effective and instead developed torpedo tube launched mines. The inclusion of airplanes on submarines was deemed unnecessary due to their limited offensive capabilities.*

BODY-67 *The V-5 and V-6 submarines were considered unweildy but completed multiple war patrols and sank 13 enemy ships. They were later used for covert troop and equipment transport before being decommissioned.*

BODY-68 *The Submarine Officer Conference (SOC) was established in 1926 to provide submarine expertise to the General Board. The lack of direct submarine experience led to flawed decisions, such as pushing for fleet speeds that were unattainable at the time. The SOC advocated for more endurance and better habitability, eventually becoming influential in the Board's decisions.*

BODY-69 *The S-class submarines had limited range and were not suitable for offensive operations against Japan in War Plan Orange. Suggestions to modify the submarines or build a fuel tender were considered but ultimately not implemented due to cost and practicality concerns.*

BODY-70 *The V-class submarines had numerous problems including low speed, poor sea keeping qualities, and engine failures. These issues made them unfit for war purposes and unable to fulfill the requirements of War Plan Orange.*

BODY-71 *US submarines in the 1920s had speed and endurance issues. The S-class could not sustain speeds above 10 kts, while the V-class had problems operating in rough seas. Additionally, there was no way to determine how much fuel remained, reducing submarine endurance.*

BODY-72 *V-class submarines had issues with fuel tanks filled with seawater, making it difficult to determine fuel levels. Lubricating oil usage was higher than predicted, limiting endurance. V-class submarines took three years to build, and the Navy preferred government shipyards over private ones for better control.*

BODY-73 *The state of the submarine force in 1927 was poor and demanded a change in design policy. The V-class submarines were expensive and had limited numbers, causing problems with replacement parts and training. The Board sought to build a cheaper and standardized submarine based on successful German U-boats.*

BODY-74 *The page discusses the challenges and specifications for building a new submarine, including incorporating lessons from previous designs and meeting war plan requirements. It also addresses concerns about the aging U.S. submarine fleet and the effectiveness of high-speed submarines in tactical cooperation with the fleet.*

BODY-75 *The page discusses the design choices and challenges faced by the US Navy in building smaller submarines with reliable diesel engines in the late 1920s.*

BODY-76 *The U.S. struggled to produce reliable diesel engines for submarines due to the unique challenges of operating in a confined space and the lack of experience in manufacturing such engines. German diesels were found to be better designed and more advanced.*

BODY-77 *The page discusses the problem of torsional vibrations in submarine engines and proposes using electric motors as a solution. However, this configuration had not been attempted before and no engines existed.*

BODY-78 *The page discusses the advantages of using diesel electric propulsion in submarines, including increased reliability and power.*

BODY-79 *The challenges of developing diesel electric propulsion for submarines in the 1920s, including the need for more powerful engines and testing on older submarines.*

BODY-80 *Diesel electric engines should be retrofitted on S-class boats instead of being installed on V-class boats, according to BuEng in 1928. The only missing component for diesel electric propulsion was a high-speed diesel engine.*

BODY-81 *The page discusses the development and success of diesel electric propulsion in submarines during World War II, highlighting its advantages in reliability and speed. It also mentions the potential for commercial applications and the involvement of various engine makers in its development.*

BODY-82 *The Board played a significant role in the development of diesel-electric submarines by holding hearings and putting pressure on BuEng to solve the propulsion problems. Their contribution was less overt but likely just as important as BuEng's in developing a reliable solution.*

BODY-83 *The V-7 submarine was a smaller and more efficient design influenced by German submarines. The 1930 London Treaty further emphasized the need for reduced submarine size to maximize fleet tonnage while maintaining capabilities for War Plan Orange.*

BODY-84 *The impact of the London treaty on the Navy's submarine building program was discussed, with options for building smaller coastal defense submarines or larger fleet submarines. The larger submarines were discounted due to their complexity and limited torpedo tubes. Small S-class submarines were also considered but lacked the range required for Pacific operations.*

BODY-85 *The page discusses the decision to build midsized submarines in order to maximize numbers and retain necessary capabilities, due to limitations imposed by the London treaty. It also mentions the construction of the last two V-class submarines, V-8 and V-9, which included various innovations.*

BODY-86 *The V-8 and V-9 submarines were innovative but too small, limiting their speed, endurance, and weapon load. They used a German diesel engine that had torsional vibration problems.*

BODY-87 *The page discusses the decommissioning of V-8 and V-9 submarines in 1945 and the Navy Department's warning about making them too small. It also mentions the deficiencies of V-5 submarine, including poor ventilation and excessive heat.*

BODY-88 *The page discusses the issue of heat inside submarines and the decision to include air conditioning units. It also mentions the debate over the number of torpedo tubes on submarines and the improvement in offensive capabilities.*

BODY-89 *The page discusses the challenges faced by submarines in the 1920s and 1930s, including difficulties in torpedo accuracy and communication. It also mentions the development of a torpedo data computer that improved torpedo fire control. The submarines designed during this period were not successful operationally, but the Board deserves credit for experimenting with different designs.*

BODY-90 *The V-class submarines provided valuable lessons for the Navy and paved the way for successful submarine designs. The implementation of diesel electric development was a key factor in their success.*

BODY-91 *The Board's pressure on BuEng led to reliable and advanced submarine propulsion in WW II. They pushed for the best designs and even explored failed technology, positively impacting submarine design from 1922-1932.*

BODY-92 *The Board was warned about small submarines in 1930 and by 1933, they were receiving complaints about lack of space. The Bureau of Construction and Engineering requested a change in submarine characteristics. RADM Land believed that a 1,500 ton submarine would be better for meeting requirements.*

BODY-93 *The page discusses the increase in size and capabilities of submarines after the London Treaty, specifically focusing on the Porpoise class submarines built in 1934.*

BODY-94 *The Porpoise class submarines were larger than previous models, but still had issues with the size of the forward torpedo room. The Perch class, similar to the Porpoise class, was the first to have air conditioning and consisted of six submarines. Some sources consider it part of the Porpoise class.*

BODY-95 *The Porpoise and Perch classes had similar offensive armament to the V-boats, with four bow torpedo tubes, two stern torpedo tubes, 16 torpedoes, and one 3 inch deck gun. They were smaller but still successful in meeting the Board's specifications for multi-ship per year build.*

BODY-96 *The P-class submarines were successful in combat during WWII, with an endurance of 11,000 nm and the ability to operate in the Pacific theater. They marked a turning point where capable submarines became the norm, thanks to advancements in propulsion and sonar technology.*

BODY-97 Sonar technology advanced during WW II, improving submarines' offensive capabilities by providing early warning and targeting data. The Board monitored the development of sonar and recognized its utility on submarines. The proposed characteristics for the next submarine class were discussed in 1935.

BODY-98 The page discusses the evolution of submarine design and the use of composite propulsion systems to improve efficiency and functionality.

BODY-99 The page discusses the propulsion system and unique features of the Salmon class submarines, including two diesel engines connected to a hydraulic clutch and four torpedo tubes on both the front and back.

BODY-100 The page discusses the TDC fire control system and the endurance of submarines, particularly in terms of battery capacity for submerged operations. The Salmon class had increased battery capacity to stay submerged for 48 hours at a slower speed.

BODY-101 The page discusses the decision to shift submarine propulsion from composite power plants to all diesel-electric designs due to concerns about vulnerability and complexity. It also mentions the importance of surface speed in submarines and how it became a priority again once diesel electric propulsion was proven successful.

BODY-102 Commander Lockwood recommends higher surface speeds for submarines in order to keep up with the fleet and attack merchant ships. The Sargo class submarines were built to achieve a sustained surface speed of 17 knots.

BODY-103 The page discusses the success of the Salmon and Sargo classes of submarines in World War II and their decommissioning by 1948. It also highlights the shift in priorities for submarine characteristics, with reliability, habitability, and endurance becoming more important than operating with the fleet.

BODY-104 In 1937, feedback on the Porpoise class submarines was positive and construction was underway for the Salmon class. Minor changes were suggested by submariners, such as increasing the number of torpedo tubes and improving habitability.

BODY-105 CDR Lockwood emphasized the importance of having multiple bow and stern torpedo tubes on submarines. The Tambor submarine was equipped with six bow and four stern torpedo tubes, as well as a 5-inch gun for potential future use in economic warfare. The larger deck guns proved useful against lightly armed ships. However, there were still limitations to the offensive capabilities of submarines.

BODY-106 Torpedo accuracy decreased with range, as shown by test data. Firing at ranges over 1000 or 1200 yards was deemed unjustified. Carrying more torpedoes improved submarines' impact and endurance in war. The U.S. submarine force had matured by the late 1930s.

BODY-107 The influence of the submarine force on the Board increased during the interwar period, with commanders and captains who had spent their entire careers in submarines providing recommendations. The Submarine Officers Conference became more influential and eventually rubberstamped many submariner recommendations. The importance of knowledgeable and mature submarine leadership on the Board cannot be understated.

BODY-108 The page discusses the Tambor class submarines, which were built according to specifications in 1939. These submarines were successful in World War II, with one boat sinking the most enemy vessels. Rear Admiral Hart, who had extensive experience with submarines, played a significant role in submarine development and served as Chairman of the Board.

BODY-109 RADM Hart's arrival on the Board brought changes to the direction of submarines, with SOC recommendations no longer being rubber stamped. RADM Hart advocated for smaller coastal submarines and the SOC supported this view, stating that the needs of the submarine service were best met by submarines of a certain type.

BODY-110 RADM Hart ordered studies on the feasibility of smaller submarines, despite initial opposition. The purpose and design of these submarines were not clearly agreed upon.

BODY-111 RADM Hart advocated for smaller submarines despite opposition, leading to the construction of two small submarines with a surfaced displacement of 800 tons.

BODY-112 The Mackerel and Marlin submarines were not successful due to their limited range and inability to be used independently. They were primarily used for training and were scrapped after World War II. Building these smaller submarines did not hinder the construction of larger fleet submarines.

BODY-113 The page discusses the development and issues with the Mark XIV torpedo, including its new magnetic influence exploder and lack of testing, which had a negative impact on submarine designs and the Pacific War effort.

BODY-114 The Mark 14 torpedo had numerous problems during WW II, with many failing to explode. Submarines were sent to war with a defective weapon, and the issue was not acknowledged by BuOrd.

BODY-115 The Mark 14 torpedo had several problems during WW II, including operating deeper than set, premature firing, circling back towards the submarine, and failure to explode. RADM Lockwood modified the exploders, resulting in successful patrols and enemy ship destruction.

BODY-116 The Mark 14 torpedo had initial faults, but after corrections, it performed well in WW II. The U.S. submarine force sank many ships using these torpedoes.

BODY-117 The page discusses the blame placed on BuOrd for the Mark 14 torpedo problems in World War II, with historians criticizing their slow investigation and failure to issue warnings.

BODY-118 The Board's relationship with the Bureaus is explored, suggesting that the Board likely knew about the lack of testing on the Mark 14 torpedo. However, there is no direct evidence linking the Board's decisions to the torpedo's failure. The Gato class submarines were built with ten torpedo tubes based on a recommendation from personnel present at a hearing.

BODY-119 The page discusses the decision to include ten torpedo tubes on the Gato class submarines and the effectiveness of submarine deck guns in World War II.

BODY-120 The Gato class submarine was an impressive ship with advanced offensive capabilities, including sonar and radar. It had 10 torpedo tubes and a deck gun, making it well-suited for War Plan Orange. The Gato class weighed 1,526 tons and could reach speeds of 21 knots on the surface.

BODY-121 The page discusses the improvements made to the high speed diesel-electric propulsion system in submarines during World War II, solving previous problems and increasing reliability. It also mentions the danger of depth charges and the importance of remaining undetected and at a different depth to increase survival chances.

BODY-122 The page discusses the importance of test depth for submarines and how increasing it improved their chances of diving under depth charges during World War II. The Gato class had a test depth of 300 feet, while the subsequent Balao class had a test depth of 400 feet. The increased depth range decreased the effectiveness of depth charges and saved many submarines from being destroyed.

BODY-123 The Board of Submarine Design significantly contributed to the production of reliable and powerful submarines required for War Plan Orange, with improvements made to *the V-class submarines. The P-class submarines marked a turning point where capable submarines became the norm.*

BODY-124 *The Gato class submarines, designed with the help of the General Board of the Navy, were praised for their standardization and suitability for Pacific warfare in World War II. Despite some flaws, they were considered the right submarines for the job.*

BODY-125 *The Board of submarine specifications had a positive influence on interwar submarine design, leading to significant advancements in U.S. submarines from WWI to WWII. While some questionable actions were taken, overall the Board was successful in shaping submarine capabilities and serving as a forum for influential experts.*

BODY-126 *The page discusses the impact of submarine design and operations on speed, endurance, habitability, and offensive armament during the interwar period. The Board focused on developing reliable propulsion for maximum surface speed but faced challenges with diesel technology.*

BODY-127 *The Board determined that maximum speed was not the most important characteristic for submarines during the interwar period. They focused on improving endurance and habitability, eventually leading to the development of a reliable diesel-electric system with a surface speed of 21 kt by the start of WW II.*

BODY-128 *The Board made significant improvements to the habitability and endurance of submarines during the interwar period, including adding air conditioning and increasing the number of torpedo tubes. These enhancements greatly impacted submarine operations in World War II.*

BODY-129 *During the interwar period, submarines had smaller deck guns, but the decision to include a 5-inch gun on the Gato class proved beneficial in sinking small Japanese ships. The Board's decisions and oversight led to significant improvements in speed, endurance, habitability, and offensive armament.*

BODY-130 *The page discusses the relationship between surface displacement and submarine size during the interwar period, highlighting the increase in size from the S-class to V-4 submarines. The Board's decision to reduce the size of later submarines was criticized for being too limiting. Additional features added weight and increased submarine effectiveness.*

BODY-131 *The Board of experts made informed decisions and influenced submarine design by bringing together experienced submariners. As the submarine force matured, the Board's knowledge increased, leading to better designs. The Board also discussed Navy policy and strategy, including using submarines in war against Japan.*

BODY-132 *The Board's discussions on submarines influenced strategy and design decisions. Further research is needed to determine the Board's role in preventing issues with the Mark 14 torpedo, as well as exploring the relationship between the SOC and the Board.*

BODY-133 *The Board and Bureaus made significant contributions to submarine design in the interwar period despite limited resources, leading to innovative solutions and advancements in submarine characteristics.*

BODY-134 *The glossary provides definitions for terms such as diesel electric, interwar, knots, nautical mile, U-boat, and submarine.*

BODY-135 *This page provides a list of interwar U.S. submarines, including their dates of commissioning, surface displacement, speed, endurance, torpedo tubes, guns, and test depth.*

BODY-136 *A list of all U.S. submarines made prior to WWI through the USS Balao.*

BODY-137 A list of submarine names and numbers.

BODY-139 This page contains a bibliography of archival sources, published primary sources, articles, and memoirs related to naval history and submarines.

BODY-140 A list of books and theses on submarine design, development, and naval history during World War I and the interwar period.

BODY-141 The page contains a list of articles and lectures about submarine policy in the United States Navy, torpedo troubles during World War II, and U.S. submarines in World War I.

BODY-142 Initial distribution list for a document, including various military institutions and individuals.

NOTABLE PASSAGES

BODY-4 *"The United States submarine force underwent significant improvement between the two world wars. In World War I, United States' submarines sank no enemy ships. A little over 20 years later the United States' submarine force crippled Japan's war efforts."*

BODY-13 *"The United States (U.S.) submarine force saw significant changes between World War I (WW I) and World War II (WW II). From a small coastal force that sank no ships in WW I to a successful long range fleet that choked Japan's supply lines and greatly contributed to victory in the Pacific, the changes in submarines were significant."*

BODY-14 *"At best most of the submarines of the 1914 vintage [those that fought WW I] and earlier were small, compared to the crews, less than a year of operations in the war and facing an enemy who wrote the book on WW I submarine tactics."*

BODY-16 *"The Board included mid grade and senior officers, whose expertise and individuality contributed to innovative solutions. As with any collection of naval officers, each member had biases based on their warfare specialty and operational experiences. The Navy's officer corps had around 7,000 men. Promotions were slow and generally only Naval Academy officers promoted to high ranks. This small number meant that by the time officers reached the rank when they could first be on the Board they knew each other and worked well together."*

BODY-19 *"Our gallant submarine personnel filled the breach after Pearl Harbor, and can claim credit, not only for holding the line, but also for carrying the war to the enemy while our shattered forces repaired damages."*

BODY-20 *"Comprising only 1.6 % of the Navy's personnel strength sank 55% of all Japanese tonnage that the United States sent to the bottom. . . . This was all the more remarkable for a force whose prewar doctrine and training had not prepared it for the war it actually fought and which for almost two years fought with a grossly defective weapon."*

BODY-22 *"Most of the information on the Board was from Agents of Innovation: The General Board and the Design of the Fleet that Defeated the Japanese Navy by John T."*

BODY-26 *"The discussion was mostly an unremarkable trip report that concentrated on the technical specifications of Britain's submarine fleet. However, the underlying message of CDR Boyd's questioning was that the U.S. submarine force would not be able to immediately make the impact of the British and especially the Germans in the war."*

BODY-27 *"It is important to understand how experts, like LT Pierce, shaped the Board's perception of the U.S. submarine's poor performance in WW I, since most submarine operations were conducted by foreign navies."*

BODY-28 *"The British are undoubtedly very much pleased with our 'H' boats which were built here and equipped with British machinery. I talked with officers who had operated these boats in the Dardanelles and also with officers in the Admiralty, and all are very enthusiastic about the American boat."*

BODY-29 *"Why, with the ability to produce a capable platform, did the U.S. not have greater success in WW I?"*

BODY-30 *"If a submarine cruising on the surface finds a German submarine, she dives and approaches as close by as possible and then fires the torpedoes at her. In the British submarine flotilla they fire about 100 torpedoes to every hit. It is very hard, of course, to hit a submarine."*

BODY-31 *"Little did the Board know that in striving for a fleet submarine, they would create a submarine that was well adapted to independent operations in support of War Plan Orange."*

BODY-32 *"The general feeling in 1917 was that the fleet submarine envisioned by the Board was neither technologically feasible nor of any operational value. In WW I, the British had an early version of a fleet submarine. During his testimony before the Board, a Royal Navy officer described these submarines as 'more submergible destroyers than large submarines. The underwater speed is very small as is their [turning] radius and they are exceedingly unwieldy.'"*

BODY-33 *"if speed in excess of twenty knots is required, it will not be possible to secure it except with steam machinery."*

BODY-34 *"CDR Land believed that the H class submarine that was well liked by the British had too many limitations for the U.S. Specifically, he wanted a submarine that could 'go to sea and keep the sea for a reasonable time.' The small 400 ton boats that made up the U.S. submarine fleet following WW I would not meet the requirements of War Plan Orange and Pacific Ocean operations."*

BODY-35 *"The Board agreed with CDR Land's assessment of the 800 ton S-class, but believed a three class strategy was required to give the Navy the required capabilities. RADM Charles J. Badger (see figure 4) described the Board's 1918 submarine building strategy. The 800-ton boat is better for offshore work, but I think the smaller boat would be better for our coast just as the conditions are near the Belgian coast. I believe in three types of boats. The large boat, the fleet boat. It is growing beyond 2000."*

BODY-39 *"The exchange showed two positive characteristics of the Board. First, the Board could bring together the best submariners of the day and allow them to directly influence design decisions. Second, the Board was willing to, when presented with a logical argument, change their original design decisions for the betterment of the fleet."*

BODY-40 *"I don't believe that there is a better diesel afloat than ours."*

BODY-41 *"We want reliability, but we want a mastery. To be conservative you do nothing except what you are perfectly sure of. The other though is to take a risk of getting something better and making some progress."*

BODY-42 *"The Board believed that one of the best ways to keep a submarine habitable was to minimize the number of crew members. Fewer sailors allowed better air quality and reduced the number of sailors sharing bunking. The problem with fewer sailors was that equipment either had to made more automatic, which usually increased complexity and reduced reliability, or off watch sailors had to be used to operate equipment, which increased operation time."*

BODY-46 *"In certain phases it would be uneconomical to keep submarines constantly with the fleet to meet a contingency which would probably not occur. It would, under normal conditions, be preferable to use these submarines to make long cruises in enemy waters, in order to act as scouts, to attack enemy naval vessels, when opportunity offers; and to prevent enemy trade to the greatest degree possible. Such an economic blockade would probably be the only way in which we could exert decisive pressure upon the enemy, and force the fleet action."*

BODY-47 *"The Board's discussion showed that the Navy was considering additional roles for submarines in a possible war against Japan as early as 1920. While it was not stated that submarines would be used to sink merchant ships in an unrestricted submarine war, the fact that submarine design was altered proved that the capability for independent submarine operations was important. In 1920 the Navy was already considering using submarines to interrupt enemy lines of communication. It should also be noted that the Board was willing to reduce speed to increase endurance, which means, while not stated, unrestricted submarine war against merchants was as important as, if not more important than, submarines operating with the fleet."*

BODY-48 *"The decision of the Navy Department to become deeply involved in submarine construction as a coordinator and catalyst proved one of its most profitable and significant policies of the 1914-1940 period."*

BODY-49 *"The response of Electric Boat to the diesel problems furthered the Navy's belief that private industry, interested in bottom lines, should not control the submarine design process."*

BODY-50 *"The poor design and reliability of U.S. submarines, specifically the S-class and the inferiority of U.S. submarines compared to the German U-boats."*

BODY-51 *"The general feeling among all respondents to the letter was that the U.S. should simply reverse engineer the German diesel engines and install them on all U.S. submarines."*

BODY-52 *"It seems to me that U-111 was designed as a war boat with a clear view of necessary qualities. The S-boats were originally designed to win the bid over the Electric Boat Company proposal in competitive trials. My opinion is that in order to eventually build successful submarines it is first necessary to destroy the wrong principles and ideas which brought forth the S-boats."*

BODY-53 *"The submariners believed that the S-class unreliable design and poor quality along with the advances that were just being understood by reverse engineering the German submarines should compel the Navy to start over."*

BODY-54 *"The submarine's principal weapon is surprise" and listed the elements of surprise as: 1. High surface speed, enabling a submarine to reach a good strategic or tactical position. 2. Quick diving qualities. 3. A most efficient listening device in order to detect surface or submerged vessels before the submarine can be sighted. 4. Long radius of action on surface and independence of outside repair facilities. 5. Weatherly qualities and good habitability, including ventilation. 6. Large radius submerged, in time more than distance."*

BODY-56 *"There was a belief in the Navy that bigger was better when it came to guns. Submarine deck guns were no exception."*

BODY-57 *"Besides reducing the size of the Navy, the Five-Power Treaty froze U.S. capital ship construction and forced the Navy and the Board to concentrate on naval aviation, smaller surface combatants, support ships and submarines."*

BODY-58 *"The impact of both the Washington treaty and the Republican Congress on submarine building was significant. From 1922 to 1932 only six submarines were built. All six were V-class submarines. For comparison, from 1912-1922, 132 submarines were built and from 1932-1942, 127 submarines were built."*

BODY-59 *"While all the 1920s submarine design decisions were not complete successes, they provided valuable lessons in submarine construction that would significantly benefit the Navy when the economic and geopolitical factors changed in the 1930s."*

BODY-60 *"The other unique mission of the V-4 was as an extended range reconnaissance platform. The submarine's planned airplane gave the submarine an over the horizon detection capability before radar existed."*

BODY-61 *"The Board's transcripts on the V-4 indicate they were trying to make a submarine that could do everything. For example, the Board envisioned the V-4 would 'lie in the enemy's trade routes and interfere with them for long periods.' This is a great mission statement for the successful WW-II Gato class, but difficult to accomplish on a submarine that has removed a significant number of."*

BODY-62 *"Argonaut was a monster, a continuous challenge, with 12 torpedoes forward, 78 mines aft, and mounting two 6-inch guns that could hurl hundred-pound projectiles nearly 20 miles."*

BODY-63 *"Argonaut's lack of air conditioning coupled with our required all-day dives resulted in ever increasing humidity and attendant electrical grounds, and fighting the ensuing small fires became almost routine."*

BODY-64 *"The Board had a unique ability to determine what design aspects were really important and press the designers to achieve the best results. The Board's primary product was a list of ship specifications, but since many of the designers were repeatedly called before the Board and, as senior leaders in the Navy, the Board could impact careers; the Board was able to ensure their wishes appeared in the built submarines."*

BODY-65 *"In previous discussions the Board continued to put new capabilities on the V-4 and by 1925 the Board recognized that a submarine with too many missions becomes less effective."*

BODY-66 *"The Germans didn't hesitate to send one across the Atlantic and do up a cruiser and bump a hole in one of our battleships."*

BODY-68 *"The lack of direct submarine experience can be seen in some of the post WW I Board's submarine decisions. In hindsight the Board's push for fleet speeds in WW I era submarines was destined to fail. The technology simply did not exist to reliably propel a submarine that fast. Looking back, ADM Galantin noted that the early V class boats were bigger and faster, but the Board fell into the shipbuilding design flaw of 'More horsepower meant more weight and space, more displacement, more fuel, more drag, more spare parts, more men, more cost, and so on.'"*

BODY-69 *"The limited range of the S-class limited it to costal defense in War Plan Orange. The S-class would not be able to conduct offensive operations against Japan until the"*

BODY-70 *"Experts told the Board that because of the S-class limitations and the V-class problems, the submarine force was not ready for 'war purpose'."*

BODY-71 *"The result was the S-class could not achieve speeds above 10 kts for any length of time. The V-class problems kept them from operating in anything but smooth water on their diesel engines. In rough seas their battery powered auxiliary engines, which only propelled the V boats at 10 kts, had to be used. The submarine force's effective speed of 10 kts would neither allow fleet action nor let submarines operate independently."*

BODY-73 *"To correct the problems the Board needed a cheaper and standardized submarine that could use economies of scale to further reduce price and increase effectiveness."*

BODY-74 *"Nothing in our experience has indicated that fleet submarines, so called, can render adequate return, for the money expended, in tactical cooperation with the fleet."*

BODY-75 *"The Navy's natural choice for more and bigger guns had to be reexamined. Rear Admiral William D. Leahy summed it up when he stated, 'Guns are heavy. The weight of the 6-inch gun is 39,800 pounds; 5-inch, 24,000 pounds, in round numbers; 4-inch, 10,000 pounds, and the 3-inch is 5,400 pounds.' The multiple 5 and 6-inch guns of the earlier V-class were no longer an option. All the remaining boats after V-6 built through the Gato class had only one gun that was less than 4-inches. Limiting weight of deck guns became a much bigger concern when designing smaller submarines*

BODY-76 *"When the U.S. examined captured German U-boats it became obvious that the German diesels were better designed and more advanced than any U.S. engines."*

BODY-77 *"In 1928 BuEng proposed to the Board using electric motors, which would not have torsional vibration problems, to provide propulsion. Separate diesel engines would be used to recharge batteries and provide electricity to the electric motors, which would in turn drive the propeller shaft. Unlike a diesel engine which provides varying torque to the propeller shaft, an electric motor provides near constant torque and does not experience torsional vibration. The problem was that the diesel electric configuration had not been attempted before and no engines existed."*

BODY-78 *"There are a great many advantages to the all-electric type of propulsion. We get away from the fact that submarines are now limited in the number of speeds at which they can run on account of critical speeds. This limitation will not apply with electric propulsion. There will be no critical speeds. All engines can be used for both charging and propulsion and there are a great many other advantages besides. But the prime advantage is that we can get more horse power and a more reliable engine in the same space than we have in the past."*

BODY-79 *"There was not a diesel engine in existence that was acceptable. There was no commercial application that would use a similar diesel engine, which meant that the cost of development would be high. Because an engine did not exist, the diesel electric engines should be put in old S boats as a test prior to installation in new submarines."*

BODY-81 *"The diesel electric configuration was exclusively used by the U.S. until 1945 and gave the U.S. submarines an advantage with reliable propulsion that was perfect for an independent deploying submarine."*

BODY-82 *"The result of the gamble was perhaps the most significant submarine development in the interwar period."*

BODY-83 *"While copying the German designs pushed the Navy towards smaller submarines, the 1930 London treaty made reducing submarine size a Board priority. The London Treaty set a limit on total submarine fleet tonnage. Most of the Board discussions in 1930 were based on designing a submarine with a weight that would maximize the number of submarines, while still retaining the capabilities necessary for War Plan Orange."*

BODY-84 *"While the numbers differed with the assumptions, most Board discussions on submarine design in 1930 had an analysis of how the future submarine's weight would fit into the London treaty. The question before the Board was now one of individual submarine size."*

BODY-85 *"Additionally, smaller submarines would not be able to go far enough from port to counter fleets using the rapidly expanding range of aircraft carrier launched airplanes."*

BODY-86 *V-8 and V-9, while innovative, were ultimately too small, which limited their speed, endurance, and weapon load.*

BODY-87 *"In cool climates the ventilation is good, in the Tropics, the heat inside the boat was almost unbearable for anything but short periods of time. Under the best Peace Time operating conditions; surface, hatches open, the temperature of the motor room was approximately 120° F."*

BODY-88 *"What I have in mind is that you can't put into fighting craft all the comforts that we might desire and in addition to that we don't consider that we would always be in tropical waters. So we must make some sort of compromise and without some comment on temperatures it would seem as if we would consider them out of all question in a boat that we would require for naval purpose."*

BODY-89 *"The TDC first appeared on the Dolphin (V-7) and would significantly enhance torpedo fire control since the CO could maneuver torpedoes instead of maneuvering the submarine."*

BODY-90 *"The second factor that should be examined is the implementation of programs and design features that would pay dividends for future submarines. First and foremost was the Navy and the Board's willingness to support diesel electric development."*

BODY-91 *"Board's continued pressure on BuEng to find a solution to submarine reliability problems, combined with the Board accepting progressive solutions to problems, led to the U.S. fielding the most reliable and advanced submarine propulsion through WW II."*

BODY-92 *"It is too tight quarters for reliability of operation, for reasonable habitability and primarily for the stowage of safety equipment that the Department requires them to carry."*

BODY-93 *"Nobody knows what tomorrow may bring."*

BODY-94 *"The Porpoise showed the Board's willingness to increase submarine size, making up for their earlier mistakes, but while the Porpoise was bigger than the last two V-class, submariners still found the forward torpedo room too small for efficient reloading and maintenance."*

BODY-95 *The Porpoise and Perch classes or P-class maintained the same offensive armament as the last two V-boats. The P-class had four bow torpedo tubes and two stern torpedo tubes. They could carry 16 torpedoes and one 3 inch deck gun. The class weighed half as much as some of the V-boats; but, with the exception of a smaller deck gun, carried a similar offensive armament. With more reliable diesels and combat multiplying auxiliary equipment, the Board's specifications for the multi ship per year build were a success.*

BODY-96 *"The P-class presented the Board with their first opportunity make a large number of submarines over a short period. In three years, there were more submarines built than there were in the previous 10 years. Incorporating the recommendations of submarine officers, the Board still built a boat that fit in the treaty restraints. The Board's insistence on BuEng correcting previous problems with propulsion finally paid off with the P-class. While the first generation diesel electric design did have problems, it proved the most reliable and advanced submarine propulsion system fielded in WW II. In judging the Board's impact on submarine design, the P-class could be seen as the turning point where capable submarines became the norm."*

BODY-97 *"The impact of sonar was significant. While WW II era sonar never advanced to the stage where a submarine could attack a target without raising a periscope, receiving early warning and additional targeting data improved a submarine's offensive capabilities."*

BODY-98 *"We were driven into the larger types by an idea that submarines would have to operate tactically on the surface with the Fleet. It was surface tactical considerations that drove us to extremes in size of submarines. The results of all the work and study that I have been able to bring to bear show that if we are going to use submarines they have got to be used in coordination with the Fleet but not in direct tactical maneuver with the Fleet. In order to do that efficiently we have to deprive ourselves of a great many features, one of which is size itself; one principal advantage of submarines lies in keeping the size down."*

BODY-100 *"By the time the Salmon class had been developed, battery capacity had increased to stay submerged for 48 hours at a slower speed of 2.5 kts."*

BODY-101 *"While surface speed was no longer the most important characteristic of submarines, it was still important. Following WW I the Board was very interested in developing a submarine that could consistently achieve greater than 21 kts to keep up with the battle fleet. Despite repeated specifications set by the Board, technology never advanced enough to produce a satisfactory propulsion system capable fleet speed. As submarine strategy evolved and treaty requirements shifted the Board to smaller submarines, surface speed became less important. Once diesel electric was proven successful, increasing surface speed again became a submarine force and Board priority."*

BODY-102 *"I was on one of those ships, the Cachalot [V-8], and by making her force speed under her engineering limitations, which was about 14.7 knots, we did reach a position ahead of the fleet but in so doing we were unable to charge batteries. . . . All of these exercises have required high surface speed and usually with the fleet submarines we have now, it has been a difficult problem to get them there in time."*

BODY-103 *"The chief characteristics of any submarines which we may build shall be first reliability, second habitability, and third endurance... then we should put in all the offensive and defensive facilities that are practicable but not at the expense of any of those three primary ones."*

BODY-104 *"Commander R. H. English, the senior member on the Porpoise's sea trials called the boat 'far superior to anything we had on our smaller submarines like the S classes.'"*

BODY-105 *"I believe that 60 per cent of those attacks are made with the bow tubes. However, with the fast zigzagging target the commanding officer can never tell definitely that he is going to attack with the bow tubes. Frequently at the last moment he is left with a situation in which he has to use the stern tubes. Therefore to have four tubes in the stern that is very important. Naturally, I would prefer to have six forward and four aft if possible."*

BODY-106 *"I don't believe that with the small numbers of torpedoes we have, firing at ranges over 1000 or 1200 yards is justified."*

BODY-107 *"The increase in the submarine force's influence on Board decision as the interwar period progressed was obvious."*

BODY-108 *"The USS Tautog, a Tambor class boat, sank 26 enemy vessels during the war, the most by any one submarine."*

BODY-109 *"It was the unanimous opinion of the Submarine Officer's Conference that the requirements for submarines as approved by the Secretary of the Navy on 17 March 1936 will be better met by a 1,450 ton submarine of the Sargo-Salmon type. . . . The Conference further feels that it is not prepared to scrap several years of progressive work and study of the Submarine Officers Conference and respectfully adheres to its former opinion that the needs of the submarine service and the requirement of the Fleet are best met by a submarine of the Salmon-Sargo characteristics."*

BODY-110 *"It seems that the General Board never came anywhere near to deciding that we should use any of our limited displacement in purely defensive types, but the agreement was easily reached that we should build as V8 and 9 the smallest boat which would answer general purposes. I don't find that those general purposes were ever very definitely agreed upon in this room or elsewhere, but the idea involved designing for long radius and protected sea."*

BODY-112 *"Their range was not sufficient for War Plan Orange. Larger fleet submarines could perform the smaller boat's mission, but the smaller boats could not be used as an independent deployer. Building the smaller submarines took a dry dock that could have been building a fleet submarine."*

BODY-113 *"The lack of testing and not aggressively finding and fixing the likely design flaws were a significant step back for the submarine force and the Pacific War effort."*

BODY-114 *"In what can only be described as a torpedo scandal, our submarines had been sent to war for 21 months with a defective weapon."*

BODY-115 *"With the modified exploder RADM Lockwood recalls that the submarine force 'made the Pacific a graveyard for enemy shipping.'"*

BODY-117 *"BuOrd's handling of the Mark 14 problems has been called 'derelict'."*

BODY-118 *"Does the Board escape all blame? To answer this question, the Board's relationship with the Bureaus should be explored. Reading the transcripts leaves little doubt that while the Bureaus did not work for the Board they had to answer the Board's questions. Had the Board insisted on more testing, it is likely that more testing would have been done. Even with the Board pressure, the secrecy of the Mark 14 torpedo might have prevented live firing exercises in the Pacific prior to the war, but at least there would have been earlier indications that the torpedo was faulty."*

BODY-119 *"The time the torpedoes are needed for counter attack is just after the submarine has made an attack on some other type of ship. He hasn't the time to get his tubes reloaded for a counter attack and I think if he has torpedoes in the tubes, both forward and aft, he is in a much better position to protect himself."*

BODY-120 *"Compared to the offensive capabilities of earlier submarines, the Gato was an impressive ship. With the evolution of sonar and the wartime development of radar, the Gato could find targets at a distance. The TDC quickly solved fire control problems allowing more torpedoes to find their mark. With 10 torpedo tubes and a deck gun, the Gato class was well adapted to the needs of War Plan Orange."*

BODY-121 *"To those of us who had grown up in submarines, where power plant breakdown were a matter of routine, with a resultant deplorable condition of engine room paint work, the spotless white-painted Fairbanks-Morse engineering spaces looked like paradise."*

BODY-122 *"You will force three different depth settings on a 600-pound charge to cover the depth range, if you can go to 300 feet. This will cause the enemy to use more depth charges. If you can only go to 250 feet, two depth settings will cover the range. 300 feet also provides increased range, in depth, for escape and a stronger hull for resistance to depth charge attack at any depth."*

BODY-123 *"combat operations had proved that the basic design of the fleet boat, although not thoroughly 'de-bugged' by war's start, was excellent for operations in the Pacific and permitted incremental improvements as combat urgencies prodded technologic progress."*

BODY-124 *"Due to conscientious work on the part of the Submarine Officers' Conference at the Navy Department, sympathetic and farsighted action by the General Board of the Navy and skillful design development on the part of the Bureau of Ships, we were able to start World War II with a standard type of Fleet submarine. This boat, with 10 tubes, 20 to 21 knots surface speed, long cruising radius and endurance, was built for just such work as was required in the Pacific. No major changes were made in it during the war."*

BODY-125 *"A good way to view the Board was as a process and forum for the most influential submarine experts. Using this paradigm, there was no doubt that the Board was a success. The Board was a clearinghouse for ideas. While the Board had no legal powers within the Department of the Navy, they held the key to determining submarine design."*

BODY-126 *"No one factor took up more of the Board's time than developing reliable propulsion that could maximize surface speed."*

BODY-127 *"The Board argued that endurance and habitability were more important and they reduced surface speed specifications for the remainder of the V-class. While reliability improved on the later V-class, diesel problems still plagued the submarine force. The Board continued to call for improvements in submarine diesels eventually pushing BuEng to work with civilian industry to develop a reliable diesel electric. By the end of the interwar period the time the Board spent on submarine propulsion had paid off."*

BODY-128 *"By increasing the number of torpedoes submarines carried the Board improved submarines' impact in War Plan Orange. Figure 23 shows the number of torpedo tubes throughout the interwar period. The Board continued to put more torpedo tubes on submarines. For a submarine operating independently, often attacking multiple targets, additional torpedo tubes were the difference between being sunk and surviving the encounter. It was interesting to note that the heaviest interwar submarine was V-4, which only had four torpedo tubes. Weighing half as much as V-4, the Gato had 10 tubes. The Navy and Board deserve credit for giving the submarines that fought WW II more than twice as much torpedo firepower without reloading as earlier submarines."*

BODY-129 *"The Board had a positive impact on surface speed, endurance, habitability and offensive Armament. The improvement in all areas was significant. The Board's decisions and the processes the Board oversaw were directly responsible for most of the advances."*

BODY-131 *"The Board had a unique ability to determine what design aspects were really important and press the designers to achieve the best results. Since many of the designers were repeatedly called before the Board and, as senior leaders in the Navy, the Board could impact careers; the Board was able to ensure their wishes appeared in the built submarines."*

BODY-132 *"The problems with the Mark 14 torpedo hurt the U.S. war efforts and cost many sailors' lives. This thesis concluded that the Board had little opportunity to prevent the issues with the Mark 14 torpedo and exploder. This conclusion was reached after a review of the Board transcripts and secondary literature."*

BODY-133 *"The Board made significant contributions to submarine design in the interwar period, a period with limited resources. While it would seem to follow that a reduction in money to build submarines and treaty limitations would cause the Board to be less innovative, the opposite was often true. Limited fiscal resources and treaty constraints forced the Board to develop innovative and unique solutions to continue the advancement of submarine design."*

THE IMPACT OF THE GENERAL BOARD OF THE NAVY ON INTERWAR SUBMARINE DESIGN

A thesis presented to the Faculty of the U.S. Army Command and General Staff College in partial fulfillment of the requirements for the degree

MASTER OF MILITARY ART AND SCIENCE
(

by

JEFFREY K JUERGENS, LCDR,USN
B.S., University of Illinois, Urbana, Illinois, 1996
M.A., Creighton University, Omaha, Nebraska, 2003

Fort Leavenworth, Kansas
2009

REPORT DOCUMENTATION PAGE	*Form Approved* *OMB No. 0704-0188*

1. REPORT DATE *(DD-MM-YYYY)*	**2. REPORT TYPE**	**3. DATES COVERED** *(From - To)*
12-06-2009	Master's Thesis	AUG 2009 – JUN 2009

4. TITLE AND SUBTITLE
The Impact of the General Board of the Navy on Interwar Submarine Design

5a. CONTRACT NUMBER

5b. GRANT NUMBER

5c. PROGRAM ELEMENT NUMBER

6. AUTHOR(S)
JUERGENS, JEFFREY K., LCDR

5d. PROJECT NUMBER

5e. TASK NUMBER

5f. WORK UNIT NUMBER

7. PERFORMING ORGANIZATION NAME(S) AND ADDRESS(ES)
U.S. Army Command and General Staff College
ATTN: ATZL-SWD-GD
Fort Leavenworth, KS 66027-2301

8. PERFORMING ORG REPORT NUMBER

9. SPONSORING / MONITORING AGENCY NAME(S) AND ADDRESS(ES)

10. SPONSOR/MONITOR'S ACRONYM(S)

11. SPONSOR/MONITOR'S REPORT NUMBER(S)

12. DISTRIBUTION / AVAILABILITY STATEMENT
Approved for Public Release; Distribution is Unlimited

13. SUPPLEMENTARY NOTES

14. ABSTRACT
The United States submarine force underwent significant improvement between the two world wars. In World War I, United States' submarines sank no enemy ships. A little over 20 years later the United States' submarine force crippled Japan's war efforts. One of the reasons was that the Navy had developed the *Gato* class submarine, which was successful independently operating in the vast Pacific Ocean in support of War Plan Orange. The group in the interwar Navy responsible for ship and submarine characteristics was a group of Admirals called the General Board of the Navy. This thesis examined the General Board of the Navy's impact on submarine design between World War One and World War Two. Using transcripts of the General Board's meetings, improvements in submarine offensive armament, propulsion, endurance and habitability were examined.

15. SUBJECT TERMS
Interwar, General Board of the Navy, Submarine, Navy, World War Two submarine operations, World War One submarine operations, War Plan Orange

16. SECURITY CLASSIFICATION OF:			**17. LIMITATION OF ABSTRACT**	**18. NUMBER OF PAGES**	**19a. NAME OF RESPONSIBLE PERSON**
a. REPORT	**b. ABSTRACT**	**c. THIS PAGE**			**19b. PHONE NUMBER** *(include area code)*
(U)	(U)	(U)	(U)	142	

Standard Form 298 (Rev. 8-98)
Prescribed by ANSI Std. Z39.18

MASTER OF MILITARY ART AND SCIENCE
THESIS APPROVAL PAGE

Name of Candidate: LCDR Jeffrey K Juergens

Thesis Title: The Impact of the General Board of the Navy on Interwar Submarine Design

Approved by:

____________________________________, Thesis Committee Chair
John T. Kuehn, Ph.D.

____________________________________, Member
Harold A. Laurence, M. P. S., M.B.A.

____________________________________, Member
Bob A. King, M.A., M.B.A.

Accepted this 12th day of June 2009 by:

____________________________________, Director, Graduate Degree Programs
Robert F. Baumann, Ph.D.

The opinions and conclusions expressed herein are those of the student author and do not necessarily represent the views of the U.S. Army Command and General Staff College or any other governmental agency. (References to this study should include the foregoing statement.)

ABSTRACT

THE IMPACT OF THE GENERAL BOARD OF THE NAVY ON INTERWAR SUBMARINE DESIGN, by LCDR Jeffrey K. Juergens, 142 pages

The United States submarine force underwent significant improvement between the two world wars. In World War I, United States' submarines sank no enemy ships. A little over 20 years later the United States' submarine force crippled Japan's war efforts. One of the reasons for this success can be attributed to the Navy's development of the *Gato* class submarine, which was successful independently operating in the vast Pacific Ocean in support of War Plan Orange. The organization in the interwar Navy responsible for ship and submarine characteristics was a group of senior officers comprising the General Board of the Navy. This thesis examined the General Board of the Navy's impact on submarine design between World War One and World War Two. Using transcripts of the General Board's meetings, improvements in submarine offensive armament, propulsion, endurance and habitability were examined.

ACKNOWLEDGMENTS

I would like to thank my thesis committee. Dr. John T. Kuehn's help and expertise in my subject were invaluable. As committee chair, he provided me the rules of the road for completing the thesis. His guidance, perspective, and positive attitude proved priceless. Mr. Harold A. Laurence and Mr. Bob A. King gave me helpful guidance while providing the necessary backup on naval and submarine issues. I would also like to thank my family. My wife Gretchen, son Garrett and daughter Olivia sacrificed to allow me to put in the required time to complete the thesis. My Mom and Dad, as always, gave their support. I hope that the work presented here is worthy of their sacrifice.

TABLE OF CONTENTS

ACRONYMS

ADM	Admiral
BuAer	Bureau of Aeronautics
BuOrd	Bureau of Ordnance
BuEng	Bureau of Engineering
BuNav	Bureau of Navigation
BuC&R	Bureau of Construction and Repair
CAPT	Navy Captain
CDR	Commander
CO	Commanding Officer
CNO	Chief of Naval Operations
kt	Knot (nautical mile per hour)
kts	Knots (nautical miles per hour)
LT	Lieutenant
LCDR	Lieutenant Commander
NIRA	National Industrial Recovery Act
nm	Nautical Mile
RADM	Rear Admiral
RPM	Revolution per minute
SLOC	Sea lines of communication
SSN	Fast attack submarine: SS denotes a submarine and the N denotes nuclear
SSBN	Ballistic missile submarine: B denotes ballistic missile
SOC	Submarine Officers Conference

TDC	Torpedo Data Computer
U.S.	United States
USN	U.S. Navy
VADM	Vice Admiral
WW	World War
XO	Executive Officer

ILLUSTRATIONS

TABLES

CHAPTER 1

INTRODUCTION

Background

The United States (U.S.) submarine force saw significant changes between World War I (WW I) and World War II (WW II). From a small coastal force that sank no ships in WW I to a successful long range fleet that choked Japan's supply lines and greatly contributed to victory in the Pacific, the changes in submarines were significant. One impetus for the change in the submarine force was a group of senior advisors to the Secretary of the Navy called the General Board of the Navy.[1] It appears that the Board's overall impact on submarine development in the interwar period was positive, even though some recommendations made by the Board had negative consequences for the submarine force. By the start of WW II, the Board's recommendations helped the U.S. create an effective submarine capable of independent operations in Japanese waters.

The submarines the U.S. sent to Europe in 1918 were inferior to the effective German U-boats. In four years the German U-boats sunk approximately 5,000 ships equating to more than 12,000,000 tons of shipping.[2] The technologically inferior U.S. submarine force did not sink a single ship in the one year it was in the war.[3] Many factors contributed to the U.S. submarines' poor record, including lack of experienced

---

[1]Hereafter referred to as the Board.

[2]Norman Friedman, *Submarine Design and Development* (London: Conway Maritime Press, 1984), 30.

[3]Edward C Whitman, "The School of War: U.S. Submarines in World War I," *Undersea Warfare* (Spring 2004), http://www.navy.mil/navydata/cno/n87/usw/issue_22/ww12.htm (accessed September 7, 2008).

crews, less than a year of operations in the war and facing an enemy who wrote the book on WW I submarine tactics. The single most problematic issue for U.S. submariners was an inferior tactical platform.[4]

The most advanced U.S. submarines used in WW I were the small K and L-classes that had a range of 3000 nautical miles at 11 knots, displaced about 450 tons on the surface and were 160 feet in length.[5] Their primary mission was targeting German U-boats on the surface while they recharged their batteries.[6] The U.S. submarines suffered from poor design choices. Because private companies conceptualized, designed and built the submarines, there was little feedback from operators into the design process. This resulted in reduced functionality of many systems and inefficient equipment placement.

U.S. submarines were not dependable. The diesel engines that were used for propulsion and recharging the batteries were so defective that many of the submarines had to be towed across the Atlantic to reach their patrol areas in the vicinity of the western approaches to the English Channel.[7] Rear Admiral (RADM) Yates Stirling summed up WW I submarine design when he stated that: “At best most of the submarines of the 1914 vintage [those that fought WW I] and earlier were small, compared to the

---

[4]Norman Friedman, *U.S. Submarines Through 1945* (Annapolis: Naval Institute Press, 1995), 159.

[5]Whitman, "The School of War: U.S. Submarines in World War I." One knot is 1.15 statute miles an hour. One nautical mile is 2000 yards. The weight of a ship measured by the weight of the amount of water it displaces. In general, a ship displaces an amount of water equal to its weight. Since a submarine ingests water into ballast tanks to submerge, a submarine has a submerged displacement that is larger than the surfaced displacement. Submerged displacement = surfaced displacement + water ingested into ballast tanks. Surface displacement will be uses as the weight of submarines.

[6]Ibid.

[7]Ibid.

giants of today [those that fought WW II], and gave the impression of being oily, greasy, unkempt conglomerations of engines, batteries, and equipment, most intricate and confusing to understand, even by experts."[8] As commander and chief of staff of the Submarine Flotilla of the Atlantic Fleet, CAPT Stirling knew at the start of WWI that the submarines were too small, unreliable and lacked trained operators.[9] In short, the offensive mission assigned to the U.S. subs in WW I was beyond their technical capacity.[10]

Post WW I reconstruction highlighted the dismal U.S. failures in submarine warfare and started discussions on how to improve. The problem was how to enact the needed changes. Private shipyard bottom lines, international treaty requirements, technological limitations, and arguments over the submarine's role in the fleet made designing submarines difficult for the Navy.

In the interwar period, the highest forum in the Navy for ship and submarine design decisions was the General Board of the Navy. Comprised of senior Admirals and their assistants, John D. Long, the Secretary of the Navy established the Board in 1900 as an advisory committee. The first chairman was the influential hero of the Battle of Manila Bay, Admiral George Dewy. As the Board matured, they gained significant influence in naval budgets, policy and strategy.[11] Additionally, the Board discussed and

---

[8]Yates Stirling, *Sea Duty: The Memoirs of a Fighting Admiral* (New York: G.P. Putnam's Sons. 1939), 154.

[9]Ibid., 155-163.

[10]Gary Weir, *Building American Submarines 1914-1940* (Washington DC: Naval Historical Center, 1991), 11.

[11]James Leutze, *A Different Kind of Victory: A Biography of Admiral Thomas C. Hart* (Annapolis: Naval Institute Press, 1981), 132.

advised on ship and system design. Josephus Daniels, Secretary of the Navy from 1913 to 1921, described the Board as "composed of officers of mature experience and eminent professional accomplishments, constituting a deliberative body to consider all matters of naval development, naval strategy, tactics, etc."[12] Since the Board influenced where the Navy spent money, the 10 years following WW I, as the Navy's budget shrank, so did the apparent influence of the Board. Still, during the 1920s, the Board was discussing the U.S. submarine problems in WW I and forging a way ahead for the submarine force.

The Board included mid grade and senior officers, whose expertise and individuality contributed to innovative solutions. As with any collection of naval officers, each member had biases based on their warfare specialty and operational experiences.[13] The Navy's officer corps had around 7,000 men. Promotions were slow and generally only Naval Academy officers promoted to high ranks. This small number meant that by the time officers reached the rank when they could first be on the Board they knew each other and worked well together.[14] The Board's members had varied experiences in the Navy that caused them to take a collaborative approach to problem solving.[15]

The Navy Bureaus were the other organization in the Navy that had tremendous influence. Prior to WW I, they controlled ship construction, resource management and

---

[12]Stephen Roskill, *Naval Policy between the Wars, Vol 1: The Period of Anglo-American Antagonism, 1919-1929* (London: Collins, 1968), 26.

[13]John T Kuehn. *The Influence of Naval Arms Limitation on U.S. Naval Innovation During the Interwar Period, 1921-1937.* PhD Thesis (Manhattan: Kansas State University, 2007) 41-42.

[14]Ibid., 43.

[15]Ibid., 42.

even policy.[16] Prior to the Board, the Bureaus reported directly to the Secretary of the Navy. Any discussions between the Bureaus were informal and disputes were resolved at the secretary level.[17] The Bureaus were seen as resistant to change, choosing instead to continue to build the last war's ships.[18] New technologies like submarines often suffered under the Bureaus. The Board provided an innovative forum to set the Navy's ship building agenda and help overcome the conservative nature of the Bureaus. As the Board matured, most of the recommendations by the Bureaus and other navy advising groups were brought before the Board for final approval. Letters from the Bureaus were routinely sent to the Board. The Board would comment on the letters and send recommendations up the Secretary of the Navy. This gave the Board the last word in navy decisions.[19] By 1922, the Board's recommendations were considered the party line for the Navy.[20]

Most major submarine design decisions were heard by the Board and their recommendations had significant influence on the decisions of civilian naval leaders. During 1917 to 1940 the Board held 57 hearings on submarines.[21] The Board would

---

[16]Ibid., 46.

[17]Ibid., 47.

[18]Friedman, *U.S. Submarine Through 1945,* 2.

[19]A review of the General Board transcripts shows that by 1917 the Bureaus had to forward major recommendations through the Board.

[20]Kuehn, *The Influence of Naval Arms Limitation on U.S. Naval Innovation During the Interwar Period, 1921-1937,* 46.

[21]*Guide to the Scholarly Resources Microfilm Edition of the Hearings before the General Board of the Navy (hereafter HBGB), 1917-50.* Lists specific topics and provides the year, volume, page number, and microfilm roll number for that topic (Wilmington, DE: Scholarly Resources, 1983), 31-33. Figure was derived by counting the number of times the guide listed a submarine topic discussed by the board. Each of these occurances produced anywhere from a couple to over 30 pages of typewritten transcripts.

often call experts before them to testify. Additionally, letters from other agencies are sometimes included in their hearing transcripts. The Board would deliberate on an issue and then send a recommendation to the Secretary of the Navy.

Another significant contribution to interwar submarine design was the U.S. Navy's preparations for an anticipated war in the Pacific. War Plan Orange was the Navy's secret strategy developed over the 40 years prior to WW II to fight Japan.[22] The plan constantly changed as the threat changed, but in general it consisted of three phases. Phase one was to ensure access to natural resources. Japan was expected to attack outlying U.S. property in the Pacific. In phase two, the U.S. would mobilize its fleet and move west to regain lost territory. The U.S. would then push forward and win a large battle between the fleets. Finally, during phase three, the U.S. would cut off Japan's resources preventing them from continuing the war through economic strangulation.[23] The submarine's role in the plan changed as they became more capable. At first submarines would be used for costal defense of U.S. outposts like the Philippines and fleet operations.[24] Additionally, the plan acknowledged that submarines could be effective commerce raiders.[25] In the interwar period, U.S. ships were designed to support War Plan Orange and the increasingly influential Board set design specifications.

By the time Japan attacked Pearl Harbor in 1941; the most modern U.S. submarines were well-suited to a wide range of operations as envisaged in War Plan

---

[22]Edward S Miller, *War Plan Orange* (Annapolis: Naval Institute Press, 1991), xix.

[23]Ibid., 4.

[24]Ibid., 57-58.

[25]Ibid., 152.

Orange. While they were not always used in the manner prescribed by War Plan Orange, the new design was precisely the sort of submarine required for the conflict that occurred.[26] Publically, the Navy intended for submarines to attack enemy warships, since submarine attacks against merchant ships had been banned in international law, but in secret discussions, including some before the Board, unrestricted submarine warfare was considered the best way to take the war to the Japanese. The horror of Pearl Harbor took public opinion out of the decision and within hours of the attack, the submarine force was ordered to commence unrestricted submarine warfare.[27] The U.S.'s unrestricted submarine campaign against Japan had devastating results. In WW II, U.S. submarines sank 1113 merchant ships, totaling 4,649,650 tons and 201 naval vessels totaling 670,444 tons.[28] Submarines were able to start phase three of War Plan Orange much earlier than anyone during the interwar period predicted and hastened the success of the plan's aim to cut off Japan's resources.[29] Admiral Chester Nimitz noted that "our gallant submarine personnel filled the breach after Pearl Harbor, and can claim credit, not only for holding the line, but also for carrying the war to the enemy while our shattered forces repaired damages."[30]

The U.S. submarines were not unopposed. The U.S. lost 52 boats and 3,506 men which were the highest per capita losses of any combat branch in the U.S. military--

---

[26]Ibid., 352.

[27]Ibid., 320.

[28]Erminio Bagnasco, *Submarines of World War Two* (Annapolis: Naval Institute Press, 1977), 213.

[29]Miller, *War Plan Orange,* 352.

[30]Charles Lockwood, *Sink 'Em All* (New York: Bantam Books, 1951), vii. From a forward written by ADM Nimitz.

Army, Navy, Air Corps, and Marines.[31] Another part of the problem was the infamous Mark XIV torpedo that did not always explode on impact. Even with the losses and weapon problems U.S. submarines were victorious. Commander Ignatius Joseph "Pete" Galantin, a future Admiral and a submarine Commanding Officer (CO) in the Pacific Fleet during WW II noted that the Submarine Force:

> Comprising only 1.6 % of the Navy's personnel strength sank 55% of all Japanese tonnage that the United States sent to the bottom. . . . This was all the more remarkable for a force whose prewar doctrine and training had not prepared it for the war it actually fought and which for almost two years fought with a grossly defective weapon. Combat operations had proven that the basic design of the fleet boat, although not thoroughly "de-bugged" by war's start, was excellent for operations in the Pacific and permitted incremental improvements as combat urgencies prodded technologic process[32]

The submarine gave the U.S. a long range independent platform to wage war on Japan's sea lines of communication (SLOC). The submarine force prevented Japan from effectively fighting the war.

Research Questions

The primary research question of this thesis was did the Board, on balance, exert a positive or negative effect on submarine design in the interwar period? What was the extent of this influence? In addressing the primary research questions, some secondary research questions were addressed. Why did the U.S. submarines perform poorly in WW I? What other factors influenced submarine construction during the interwar period?

---

[31]Clay Blair, *Silent Victory: The U.S. Submarine War Against Japan* (Annapolis: Naval Institute Press, 2001), 12.

[32]Ignatius J Galantin, *Submarine Admiral: From Battlewagons to Ballistic Missiles* (Urbana: University of Illinois Press, 1995), 122.

What effect did individual members on the Board have on submarine design? The *Gato* class submarine first put into service in the fleet was very successful. Were there any design decisions that the Board did not recommend that could have increased its war fighting capability? Did the Board understand the lack of testing of the Mark XIV torpedo that handicapped the submarine force early in WW II?

Limitations

I could not get all the official correspondences from the Board from primary sources. The Board studies on submarine design (the serials) reside in the National Archives in Washington, D.C. However, the Board hearing transcripts often give their recommendations and secondary sources covered their recommendations. Similarly, the OPNAV War Plans Division material is also in Washington, D.C. However, much of the evidence concerning War Plan Orange is covered adequately in secondary sources.

Significance

The U.S. submarine force made significant strides in the interwar period. While the Board influenced many of the submarine design decisions, there is limited literature analyzing how they influenced submarines.

Literature Review

There are numerous books, journal articles and official records on submarines. Submarine operations in both World Wars were well documented in primary sources and analyzed in secondary sources. While the interwar period had less literature than the two World Wars, there were still a number of good primary and secondary sources.

Archival records constituted a large portion of my written sources. The records of the Board during the interwar period provided most of my primary research. These transcripts included deliberations among the Board and correspondence to the Board. Additionally, other interwar Navy records were examined.

Some published primary sources were also used. Autobiographies like ADM Ignatius "Pete" Galantin's *Submarine Admiral: From Battlewagons to Ballistic Missiles*, RADM Yatets Stirling's *Sea Duty: The Memoirs of a Fighting Admiral*, ADM Charles A. Lockwood's *Down to the Sea in Subs*, and RADM Harold G. Bowen's *Ships, Machinery, and Mossbacks* provided a good first hand perspective of submarine design, development and operations of the interwar submarine fleet.

A helpful secondary source was *Building American Submarines 1914-1940* by Gary Weir. The book described the interwar development of submarines. While it provided an overview of the evolution of submarine design decisions, it also explored the Navy's relationships with industry. Weir consulted the Board's records, but did not thoroughly investigate their influence on submarine design.

Two other sources that provide a good overview of interwar submarines were *Dictionary of American Naval Fighting Ships*, a great primary source on ship histories for U.S. Navy ships and auxiliaries and Norman Friedman's very detailed *U.S. Submarines Through 1945*. Friedman's book covered the interwar submarine period in detail, using many official records, including General Board transcripts, studies (serials) and correspondences.

Most of the information on the Board was from *Agents of Innovation: The General Board and the Design of the Fleet that Defeated the Japanese Navy* by John T.

Kuehn. The book examined the influence of the Board during the interwar period. Dr. Kuehn believed that the Board acted as an agent of innovation in the years between the world wars and positively influenced the WW II fleet design. There was very little direct analysis of the Board's actions in the interwar period beyond *Agents of Innovation*. Many secondary sources acknowledged the Board's influence and make judgment on their decisions, but only *Agents of Innovation* looks specifically at their actions and what constrained them between the wars.

One secondary source, Edward S Miller's *War Plan Orange*, was used to understand War Plan Orange. The book provided a good overview of the Japanese threat to the U.S. in the interwar period and how the Navy planned to counter it. Like the Board this was one of very few sources that specifically analyzed War Plan Orange.

Research Design

There was no shortage of literature on all aspects of submarines from WW I to WW II. There was significant data on submarine specifications, mission, and strategic use. It was important to understand all the submarine design's successes and failures. Additionally, understanding why submarines evolved from a short range coastal defense platform to a capable long range independent deployer was required. Finally, the external factors, such as treaties and moral implications that altered the strategic plans for submarines and changed their specification and mission, were studied.

All the transcripts from 1917 through WW II were available via micro-film in the Combined Arms Research Library (CARL). The records were legible and generally easy to read. Included in the records were correspondences to the Board. The bulk of the research was searching these records and determining how the Board's recommendations affected submarine specifications, mission and strategic use.

To determine if the Board made a positive impact, an examination of the hearing transcripts was needed to see how their recommendations and guidance shaped the submarine force. The Board's recommendations were compared with the capabilities dictated by War Plan Orange looking at four factors. The first was speed; specifically surface speed, which allowed a submarine to quickly cross the Pacific Ocean to its patrol areas and position itself for an attack on enemy ships. The second was endurance which was a key aspect of being able to operate from U.S. bases in enemy waters. The third was submarine's armament. This was primarily an examination of torpedoes and torpedo delivery systems. Deck guns, which were used with limited success in WW II, were investigated to a lesser degree. Finally, the study examined habitability, which includes the air quality and crew comfort that was needed for long-range operations. Each of these factors was examined in discrete time frames within the interwar period.

Other very important factors that increased submarine capabilities were either not examined or only briefly discussed. These included important submarine technological advances like better periscopes because the Board did not significantly discuss them. Radar was only briefly mentioned because its employment on submarines occurred after the time frame that was evaluated.

The thesis consists of five chapters. The first chapter introduced the research question and method. Chapter 2 explores the Board and its impact on submarine development from the years 1917-1921. Chapter 3 discusses the years 1922-1932. Chapter 4 covers the years 1933-1940. Finally, Chapter 5 provided conclusions on the

Board's impact and suggested the areas for continued analysis and research raised by them.

CHAPTER 2

1917-1921

By 8 September 1917, the U.S. had been at war for five months. The submarine force prepared for its first overseas combat deployments in its young existence. Commander (CDR) D.F Boyd had just returned from a tour of Britain's submarine operations and was called before the Board to discuss his experiences and insight. Rear Admiral Albert G. Winterhalter, former commander of the U.S. Asiatic Fleet, and Rear Admiral Charles Badger, the former Commander in Chief of the U.S. Atlantic Fleet, questioned CDR Boyd on his experiences in England. The discussion was mostly an unremarkable trip report that concentrated on the technical specifications of Britain's submarine fleet.[1] However, the underlying message of CDR Boyd's questioning was that the U.S. submarine force would not be able to immediately make the impact of the British and especially the Germans in the war. The British had about 200 submarines and over three years of war experience.[2] One exchange, comparing the crews of each country, shows the disparity:

> ADMIRAL BADGER: How are the hours of the crew arranged?
>
> COMMANDER BOYD: It depends upon the station. Some go out for a week and then lay up for a week and then have a torpedo firing for the third week. That puts them at sea one-third of the time. Off the coast of Ireland they are [at] sea 12 days and in port six.
>
> ADMIRAL BADGER. Does this harden the crews so that they become accustomed to it? A green crew would suffer.

---

[1]General Board Hearings (hereafter GBH) September 8, 1917. Hearings Before the General Board of the Navy 1917-50 (hereafter HBGB), roll 1, year 1917, page 176-192.

[2]Ibid., 182.

COMMANDER BOYD: They don't have green crews. It is a volunteer service. The commodore of the submarines can take any officer or man he wants and that applies to battleships or any other kind of vessel. They are generally very able men mentally and physically.

ADMIRAL BADGER: We have had reports that in our smaller type of boat the men were seasick. We never had them out for more than a 24-hour trip. We were afraid of the demands for a larger boat for coast patrol. That doesn't work out that way in England.[3]

The lack of operational experience for the U.S. was obvious. While British crews routinely operated for 12 days at a time, U.S. crews could not consistently stay at sea for longer than 24 hours. Poor machinery reliability and habitability combined with limited crew experience meant that U.S. submarines simply were not ready for extended operations at sea.

With the U.S. behind in submarine operations, it was important for the Board to have up to date intelligence on foreign submarine fleets. On 9 October 1917, the Board brought Lieutenant (LT) M. R. Pierce before them. His description of his recent trip to England and deployment on the British submarine E-34 patrolling the North Sea and Heligoland Bight, provided excellent insight into WW I submarine operations.[4] LT Pierce's firsthand account was delivered to the Board immediately upon his return to the U.S. and within two months of his experience. His testimony showed the Board's ability to get the most up to date and relevant information on a topic.

It is important to understand how experts, like LT Pierce, shaped the Board's perception of the U.S. submarine's poor performance in WW I, since most submarine

---

[3]Ibid., 189-190.

[4]GBH October 9, 1917, HBGB, roll 1, year 1917, page 343-368. LT Pierce's account is a fascinating description of a British submarine patrol. LT Pierce stood watch and took part on a successful attack of a German ship. Additionally, his transport was attacked by a German submarine on his trip to England.

discussions before the Board in the 1920s dealt with improving the perceived WW I failures. Many submarine historians consider the U.S. submarines to be an inferior platform to the British and especially German submarines. While there certainly were problems with the U.S. submarines, some evidence presented to the Board showed the U.S. could design a successful submarine. Twice in 1917, experts praised U.S. submarines before the Board. LT Pierce stated that "The British are undoubtedly very much pleased with our "H" boats which were built here and equipped with British machinery. I talked with officers who had operated these boats in the Dardanelles and also with officers in the Admiralty, and all are very enthusiastic about the American boat."[5] To understand why the British would like the H-class, its primary mission must be understood. The H-class submarine was a submarine hunter, a smaller coastal defense boat designed to protect merchant shipping by destroying German U-boats. Lieutenant C. H. Varley of the Royal Navy explained that the most desired characteristics of a submarine hunter were a high submerged speed to covertly approach surfaced German U-boats and good submerged ship handling at periscope depth.[6] The H class boats were built in the U.S. for the British and, with a submerged speed of 10 kts and good submerged handling characteristics. The H class boat was a good start for submarine hunting. The U.S. did not field the H class during WW I. If they had, they likely would have had the same reliability problems that plagued other U.S. submarines, since they would have had U.S. made diesels instead of the more reliable foreign diesels.

---

[5]Ibid., 350.

[6]GBH December 19, 1917, HBGB, roll 1, year 1917, page 730. Periscope depth is the depth where the entire submarine is below the water except for the periscope when raised.

Photo # NH 51152 USS L-1 running trials

Figure 1. *L-1*
Source: Naval Historical Center, L-1, http://www.history.navy.mil/photos/images/h51000/h51152.jpg (accessed April 15, 2009).

The first U.S. submarines to serve in WW I were the L-class boats (see figure 1), which arrived in Ireland in January 1918. They conducted anti-submarine patrols around Ireland until the end of the war in November.[7] The L-class was an improved version of the H-class boat that Britain held in such high regard. Why, with the ability to produce a capable platform, did the U.S. not have greater success in WW I? First, the engines of

[7]Whitman, "The School of War: U.S. Submarines in World War I."

U.S. subs in K and L-classes were unreliable.[8] So unreliable, that the K-class (see figure 2), while deployed to the Azores, rarely left port.[9] Second, the U.S. crews lacked wartime experience.[10] Third, the anti-submarine mission assigned to the U.S. was a very difficult mission. Even the British, with years of wartime experience, were not proficient. In his testimony before the Board, LT Pierce stated that,

> If a submarine cruising on the surface finds a German submarine, she dives and approaches as close by as possible and then fires the torpedoes at her. In the British submarine flotilla they fire about 100 torpedoes to every hit. It is very hard, of course, to hit a submarine.[11]

As WW I came to an end, naval aviation was becoming more proficient at anti-submarine warfare, which kept many of the U-boats in port and limited the potential number of targets for U.S. submarines.[12] Finally, U.S. submarines were only in WW I for 11 months, thus limiting the number of opportunities to sink enemy ships and preventing the crews from building the necessary experience level. With the mechanical problem, difficulty of the mission, lack of experience and short time in the war it was little surprise that the U.S. did not achieve successes in WW I. The Board understood most of the problems that faced the WW I submarine force and looked to change submarines from a

---

[8]Friedman, *U.S. Submarine Through 1945,* 77. The switch was made to be able to reverse directions on the engine. The 1910 Board made the change from a 4-cycle engine to a 2-cycle engine due to some engineering problems. Also, GBH 8 Sep 1917. HBGB, roll 1, year 1917, page 320. LT Pierce states "The engines are the principal defects of our boats." Additionally, he discusses the British use of a 4-cycle engine for reliability. The U.S. used a 2-cycle engine. The British used 2 cycle engine in experimental boats, but were unable to make them reliable.

[9]Whitman, "The School of War: U.S. Submarines in World War I."

[10]GBH September 8, 1917, HBGB, roll 1, year 1917, page 189-190. This is the discussion with CDR Boyd and the Board.

[11]GBH October 9, 1917, HBGB, roll 1, year 1917, page 345.

[12]Paul G. Halpern. *A Naval History of World War I* (Annapolis: Naval Institute Press, 1994) 441.

costal defense platform to an asset that could steam and fight with the rest of the battle fleet. Little did the Board know that in striving for a fleet submarine, they would create a submarine that was well adapted to independent operations in support of War Plan Orange.

Figure 2. K-4
Source: Naval Historical Center, K-4, http://www.history.navy.mil/photos/images/h41000/h41963.jpg (accessed April 15, 2009).

Steam Powered Submarines

The lessons of WW I along with a feeling in the Navy that Japan was the next opponent shaped the Board's submarine building recommendations. Throughout the

Board's submarine discussions in 1917, there was a desire by the leadership to investigate the feasibility of a larger steam driven submarine to operate with the fleet.[13] A fleet submarine would scout ahead of a group of battleships, and if needed conduct attacks against enemy warships. One of the biggest challenges to overcome in the development of the fleet submarine was increased speed to keep up with the faster surface ships and improved ability to withstand longer deployments. Every submarine expert brought before the Board was asked about the prospect of building and fielding a large (2000 ton) fleet submarine. The general feeling in 1917 was that the fleet submarine envisioned by the Board was neither technologically feasible nor of any operational value. In WW I, the British had an early version of a fleet submarine. During his testimony before the Board, a Royal Navy officer described these submarines as "more submergible destroyers than large submarines. The underwater speed is very small as is their [turning] radius and they are exceedingly unwieldy."[14] Despite the potential problems, the Board made a recommendation for 30 fleet submarines.[15] The debate of whether to build a large fleet submarine or a small coastal defense platform continued to occur before the Board until WW II.[16] In fact, many of the best characteristics of small costal defense submarines and

[13]Throughout the GBH 1917, HBGB, roll 1, year 1917, there are discussions of a larger fleet submarine.

[14]GBH December 19, 1917, HBGB, roll 1, year 1917, page 747.

[15]GBH February 27, 1918, HBGB, roll 1, year 1918, page 363.

[16]RADM HART was pushing for a small boat in the late 30's.

the larger fleet submarines went into the design of the successful WW II *Gato* and *Balao* class submarines.[17]

In 1918, the discussion of the feasibility of a steam powered submarine continued. The Submarine Design Board believed that the size required to house a steam power plant would "result in a craft that under water will be neither safe nor effective."[18] They recommended that, "steam be not used for submarines of the current program, and be not attempted at any time unless a design be produced that is much more promising than any now available. Diesel engine propulsion is recommended for the fleet submarine and others projected."[19] The Bureau of Steam Engineering reported that "if speed in excess of twenty knots is required, it will not be possible to secure it except with steam machinery."[20] The conclusion that submarines could not reach the required speed without steam propulsion, which was not recommended, put the Board's plans on hold. Instead, the Board recommended building nine larger submarines with diesel engines knowing that the goal was a submarine to operate at fleet speeds to fulfill the requirements of War Plan Orange.[21] The nine submarines would become the V-class, which was the Navy's first attempt at a fleet submarine.[22] It is to the Board's credit that once they heard the evidence that a steam driven submarine was determined to be technologically infeasible

[17]The WWII Gato and Balao class submarines were often called fleet submarines because of their ability to make fleet speeds, but they generally operated independently and, based on their mission, were not what the Board in 1917 would have called a fleet submarine.

[18]GBH December 20, 1918, HBGB, roll 1, year 1918, page 1357.

[19]Ibid.

[20]Ibid., 1358.

[21]GBH February 17, 1919, HBGB, roll 2, year 1918, page 137.

[22]Bagnasco, *Submarines of World War Two,* 217.

they changed their position shifting to diesel propulsion, but did not completely abandon the fleet submarine.[23]

S-class

A key figure in interwar submarine development was the future Vice Admiral (VADM) Emory S. Land (see figure 3), a naval architect specializing in submarine construction. Emory Land significantly contributed to the development of the S-class submarines, the first Navy designed submarine and a step in the evolution of the fleet submarine.[24] On 27 February 1918 then CDR Land appeared before the Board and discussed his opinions on submarine size. CDR Land believed that the H class submarine that was well liked by the British had too many limitations for the U.S. Specifically, he wanted a submarine that could "go to sea and keep the sea for a reasonable time."[25] The small 400 ton boats that made up the U.S. submarine fleet following WW I would not meet the requirements of War Plan Orange and Pacific Ocean operations.

---

[23]The successful WW II *Gato* class had a displacement of approximately 1500 tons. The discussion of submarine size in the interwar period is an important one. Generally, as displacement increases so does size. A larger submarine is required to house equipment and stores for long deployments; comfortably transports the larger crew required to operate the additional equipment; store more torpedoes; and carry a diesel engine large enough to achieve the required speed.

[24]Division, Chief of Naval Operations Submarine Warfare. *Submarine Pioneers Biographies.* http://www.navy.mil/navydata/cno/n87/history/pioneers4.html#Emory%20Scott%20Land (accessed October 4, 2008).

[25]GBH February 27, 1918, HBGB, roll 2, year 1918, page 369.

Figure 3. VADM Emory S. Land
Source: U.S. Navy, VADM Emory S. Land, http://www.navy.mil/navydata/cno/n87/images/land.jpg (accessed April 15, 2009).

The Board agreed with CDR Land's assessment of the 800 ton S-class, but believed a three class strategy was required to give the Navy the required capabilities. RADM Charles J. Badger (see figure 4) described the Board's 1918 submarine building strategy.

> The 800-ton boat is better for offshore work, but I think the smaller boat would be better for our coast just as the conditions are near the Belgian coast. I believe in three types of boats. The large boat, the fleet boat. It is growing beyond 2000

> tons. I believe in the 800 ton boat for offshore work in more or less deep water. I believe in the 400-500-ton for inshore.[26]

The Navy had small 400-500 ton submarines following the build up for WW I. The Board had developed initial specifications for a fleet submarine that would be debated as the operational fleet and the Bureaus advised the Board on technological and operations feasibility. The soon to be commissioned S-class would provide a submarine for offshore operations and bridge the gap between costal defense and fleet submarines.

REAR ADMIRAL
CHARLES J. BADGER

Figure 4. RADM Charles J. Badger
Source: Arlington National Cemetery, RADM Charles J. Badger, http://www.arlingtoncemetery.net/cjbadger.htm (accessed April 15, 2009).

The S-class was designed prior to the start of WW I and the first entered the fleet in 1920.[27] The S-class was a response to 800 ton German submarines that could

[26]Ibid., 370.

successfully operate around England from their home ports in Germany. With a planned surface speed of 15 knots; 5000 nm endurance; submerged speed up to 14 kts for 1 hour or 5 kts for 20 hours; and four bow torpedo tubes, the 51 ship S-class made up the bulk of the interwar submarine fleet.[28] While the S-class was a step forward, it had many problems. S-class boats were not ready to be an independent deployer because of unreliable diesel engines and poor habitability in hot environments.[29] Once the U.S. finally got to examine captured WW I U-boats, U.S. submariners realized the S boats (see figure 5) were inferior to the German submarines in most respects.[30] Much of the interwar period was spent correcting the design problems of the S-class, while moving towards a fleet submarine.

The S-class was the first submarine that was designed by the Navy. The class was broken into four groups depending on who built them.[31] The basic specifications were set, but there were differences including different installed machinery including the diesel engines. All the S-class boats were built between 1918 and 1924.[32] The class served in WW II, largely as a training platform and in a costal defense role, and had been retired from Navy service by 1946.[33]

---

[27]Friedman, *U.S. Submarine Through 1945,* 117.

[28]Ibid., 308-309.

[29]Weir, *Building American Submarines 1914-1940,* 42.

[30]Ibid., 28-29.

[31]Friedman, *U.S. Submarine Through 1945,* 290-292. Group I: S-1 and S-18 through S-41, built by subcontractors for Electric Boat. Group II: S-3 through S-17, built at the Portsmouth Navy Yard. Group III: S-42 through S-47, built at Fore River. Group IV: S-48 through S-51, built by Lake Torpedo Boat.

[32]Ibid.

[33]Ibid.

Photo # NH 99772 USS S-1 underway during trials, circa April 1920

Figure 5. *S-1*
Source: Naval Historical Center, *S-1,* http://www.history.navy.mil/photos/images/h99000/h99772.jpg, (accessed April 15, 2009).

Technological Problems with Fleet Submarine Specifications

In 1919, U.S. submariners had toured captured German submarines and the Bureaus had completed further studies of the Board's request for fleet submarines. The two groups came together before the Board and set the specifications for the Navy's first attempt at a large fleet submarine.

1. Armament: Two 5 inch deck guns, one 3 inch anti aircraft gun, four 21 inch bow torpedo tubes and one 21 inch broad torpedo tube.
2. Propulsion: Surface speed 25 knots
3. Endurance: Radius of 6000 nautical miles nominal and 10000 nautical miles maximum at 11 knots.[34]

[34]GBH February 6, 1919, HBGB, roll 2, year 1919, page 62.

These three specifications, set by the Board, were the basis for most of the discussion in 1919.

Of the three areas, no changes were as big as those made in armament. There was little debate about the four bow tubes, but the single broadside tube brought considerable discussion. In one discussion, three future Admirals were brought before the Board to express their opinion on the broadside tubes. CAPT Hart informed that Board that construction of a submarine with broad side tubes was difficult and that there was no tactical advantage to be had. Commander Chester Nimitz and CDR Land agreed with CAPT Hart's assessment.[35] The three went on to express their desire for the requirement to be shifted to two stern tubes.[36] The Board agreed on both accounts and changed the specifications to four bow tubes and two stern tubes, which eventually evolved into the six bow and four stern tubes on the newest WW II production submarines. The exchange showed two positive characteristics of the Board. First, the Board could bring together the best submariners of the day and allow them to directly influence design decisions. Second, the Board was willing to, when presented with a logical argument, change their original design decisions for the betterment of the fleet.

Similar discussions were conducted with CAPT Hart, CDR Nimitz and CDR Land on submarine guns. Once again, the Board was willing to change their initial specifications and eliminate an anti-aircraft gun that German experience indicated was

---

[35]GBH February 17, 1919, HBGB, roll 2, year 1919, page 120.

[36]Ibid., 121-122.

useless.[37] The deck gun was discussed and consensus was reached on one instead of two, but the size and placement continue to be debated.[38]

With the Board realizing the technological problem with steam propulsion, the discussion shifted to a reasonable expectation for surfaced speed using diesel. Inspection of captured German WW I U-boats confirmed what many already believed, that German diesel engines were superior.[39] The best German U-boats made 15.5 to 17 knots.[40] ADM Winterhalter stated that the Board "want 25 knots" for U.S. submarines.[41] The Board was told that the U.S. could develop a diesel that would power a 2,000 ton submarine to 18 knots on the surface.[42] ADM Dyson commented "I don't believe that there is a better diesel afloat than ours."[43] The Board overestimated U.S. diesel technology. The submarine diesel continued to be a problem throughout the 1920s. Was the Board's overestimation of U.S. industrial capabilities a detriment to the evolution of the interwar submarine? There are two ways to look at it. First, the weakness of WW I submarines was their diesel engine. Those problems continued with the S-class.[44] The Board knew the diesel was a problem and should have moved to fix it, instead of assuming the problems would be worked out. They were relying on emerging

---

[37]Ibid., 116.

[38]GBH March 3, 1919, HBGB, roll 2, year 1919, page 146-148.

[39]GBH February 6, 1919, HBGB, roll 2, year 1919, page 67.

[40]Ibid., 69.

[41]Ibid., 83.

[42]Ibid., 95.

[43]Ibid.

[44]Weir, *Building American Submarines 1914-1940,* 28.

technology, a poor practice that the Board continued to use until the early 1930s and the development of the diesel electric drive.

Second, while it is hard to say the Board's confidence in diesel technology was well founded, they did not allow technological problems with diesel engines to slow the development of submarines. It would have been easy for the Board to say that we could not make a diesel to drive a 1,500 ton submarine and give up on bigger submarines. Eventually, with Board guidance, the diesel problem was corrected. ADM Winterhalter realized there could be a problem with the proposed diesel, but accepted the risk when he stated, "We want reliability, but we want a mastery. To be conservative you do nothing except what you are perfectly sure of. The other though is to take a risk of getting something better and making some progress."[45]

There was a direct relationship between endurance and propulsion. Speed is achieved by building larger and more powerful diesel engines, which burn more fuel, reducing their endurance. CDR Land described the Board endurance specification as "an impossible proposition at the time."[46] The Board finally settled on the non-specific best range possible, while indicating that a range under the S-class's 5,000-6,000 nm was unacceptable.[47]

With the requirement of longer ranges, came the need for better habitability. Because of high heat, poor air quality and cramped living conditions, habitability was poor on WW I submarines. However, short patrols made it tolerable for the crew.

[45]GBH February 7, 1919, HBGB, roll 2, year 1919, page 96.

[46]GBH February 6, 1919, HBGB, roll 2, year 1919, page 78. Radius of 6000 nautical miles nominal and 10000 nautical miles maximum at 11 knots was the Board's request.

[47]GBH February 7, 1919, HBGB, roll 2, year 1919, page 85.

Submarines to support War Plan Orange had to be different; the Pacific had large distances and tropical conditions that required habitability improvements.[48] The Board had their first discussions on submarine habitability in 1917, and set the required characteristics in 1919. The Board believed that one of the best ways to keep a submarine habitable was to minimize the number of crew members. Fewer sailors allowed better air quality and reduced the number of sailors sharing bunking. The problem with fewer sailors was that equipment either had to made more automatic, which usually increased complexity and reduced reliability, or off watch sailors had to be used to operate equipment, which increased operation time.[49] For example, the Board realized WW I crew size was inadequate to quickly dive the boat. Off watch and often asleep people were counted on to take immediate actions to dive the submarine, which slowed the dive and risked the submarine's survival.[50] The Board settled on a nominal crew size of five officers and 50 men.[51]

The Fleet Submarine Concept and the V-class

Submarines that could operate with the fleet were not a new idea. Naval strategists had always wanted a fleet submarine that could maintain pace with other warships. The primary requirements for such a submarine were surface speed of greater

---

[48]Weir, *Building American Submarines 1914-1940*, 79.

[49]GBH February 17, 1919, HBGB, roll 2, year 1919, page 107.

[50]Brayton Harris, *Submarines: A Political, Social And Military History* (New York: Berkley Books, 1997), 253.

[51]GBH February 17, 1919, HBGB, roll 2, year 1919, page 103 and GBH January 30, 1920, HBGB, roll 2, year 1920, page 103.

than 21 kts, to operate ahead of the fleet, and better armament.[52] In the early 1900s many designs were imagined, but all were not technological possible.[53] In 1913, Lawrence Y. Spear, Electric Boat's chief naval architect, submitted initial fleet submarine specifications and Congress authorized the building of one fleet submarine in 1915. [54] The first U.S. attempt at fleet submarines became the USS *Schley* (SS-52/T-1) and her sisters T-2 and T-3. With a surface displacement of 1,106 tons, the T class was twice as big as any other U.S. submarine before.[55] Unfortunately, foreshadowing fleet submarine problems to come, the T class' two directly coupled diesel engines had severe torsional vibration problems and were all decommissioned by 1923.[56]

In 1916, with the U.S. entry in WW I more likely, and before the problems with the T class became known, Congress authorized the building of nine fleet submarines.[57] The V-class was a group of nine submarines built from 1921 to 1933. They were the only submarines built from 1925 - 1934.[58] The V-class is called a class in name only because it actually consisted of five different designs under the Congressional fleet submarine building program.[59] All nine of the V-class were built by government

[52]Edward C Whitman, "The Navy's Variegated V-Class." *Undersea Warfare.* Fall 2008. http://www.navy.mil/navydata/cno/n87/usw/issue_20vclass1.htm (accessed December 18, 2008).

[53]Friedman, *U.S. Submarines Through 1945*, 100.

[54]Edward C Whitman, "The Navy's Variegated V-Class."

[55]Friedman, *U.S. Submarines Through 1945*, 309.

[56]Ibid., 288. T-3 was recommissioned in 1925 and decommissioned again in 1927.

[57]Edward C Whitman, "The Navy's Variegated V-Class."

[58]Friedman, *U.S. Submarines Through 1945*, 290-292.

[59]Edward C Whitman, "The Navy's Variegated V-Class." Called a class in name only in the article.

shipyards to improve the shipyard's experience.[60] Because such a long portion of the interwar period was spent on the V-class, the Board's impact on interwar submarine development was largely tied to the V-class. The V-class was important to the Navy's submarine development because each submarine provided valuable lessons learned that were incorporated into later submarines.

The submarines built to the 1919 specifications were the first three boats in the V-class.[61] *V-1* through *V-3, Barracuda, Bass and Bonita* respectively, were the fastest of the V-class submarines.[62] They had four diesel engines, two for surface propulsion and two to recharge the batteries. All four were directly coupled to make a maximum specified speed of 21 kts.[63] Their diesel engines were generally unreliable and the boats were much too heavy and eventually had to be overhauled to reduce their weight.[64] *V-1* through *V-3* were used for costal defense and as cargo submarines in WW II and decommissioned in 1945.[65] Figures 6 and 7 are pictures of *V-3*.

---

[60]Friedman, *U.S. Submarines Through 1945*, 290-292.

[61]Ibid., 110-113.

[62]Ibid., 290-292.

[63]Edward C Whitman, "The Navy's Variegated V-Class." They only made 18.7 kts in sea trials.

[64]Friedman, *U.S. Submarines Through 1945*, 111.

[65]Ibid., 290-292.

Figure 6. *V-3*
Source: Naval Historical Center, *V-3*, http://www.history.navy.mil/photos/images/h56000/h56511.jpg (accessed April 15, 2009).

Photo # NH 74639 USS V-3 entering Porto Bello Harbor, Panama, March 1927

Figure 7. *V-3*
Source: Naval Historical Center, *V-3*, http://www.history.navy.mil/photos/images/h74000/h74639.jpg (accessed April 15, 2009).

1920: Surface Speed or Endurance and Problems with Private Shipyards

Two issues dominated the 1920 submarine discussions before the Board. The first was a reexamination of the submarine's role in navy war plans sparked by the Board's routing of their 1919 fleet submarine characteristics to the Director of Naval Plans. The Director submitted a letter to their boss, the Chief of Naval Operations (CNO), commenting on the Board's recommendations. The letter requested that "in the design of these submarines, their employment other than in fleet action should be given full consideration."[66] In describing War Plan Orange, the Director of Naval Plans stated that:

> In certain phases it would be uneconomical to keep submarines constantly with the fleet to meet a contingency which would probably not occur. It would, under normal conditions, be preferable to use these submarines to make long cruises in enemy waters, in order to act as scouts, to attack enemy naval vessels, when opportunity offers; and to prevent enemy trade to the greatest degree possible. Such an economic blockade would probably be the only way in which we could exert decisive pressure upon the enemy, and force the fleet action.[67]

The Director recommended that three fleet submarines (*V-1* through *V-3*), of the nine authorized, be constructed using the Board's 1919 fleet submarine characteristics. The remaining six would be constructed using revised specifications. The Director believed the great distances and lack of repair facilities in the Pacific demanded submarines that had a large cruising radius, reliable machinery, good habitability and excess storage.[68]

The Director's letter altered many of the fleet submarine specifications; the major debate was between endurance and surface speed. To deploy from a Pacific U.S. base,

---

[66]GBH February 4, 1920, HBGB, roll 2, year 1920, page 170.

[67]Ibid.

[68]Ibid., 169-170.

travel to Japan, and conduct operations, 20,000 nm of endurance was required.[69] Smaller efficient engines and additional fuel storage were required.[70] An additional consideration for long deployments was habitability. To improve habitability, additional space had to be allocated to crew berthing and equipment to improve crew comfort. The Board argued that endurance and habitability were more important and they reduced surface speed specifications for the remainder of the V-class.

The Board's discussion showed that the Navy was considering additional roles for submarines in a possible war against Japan as early as 1920. While it was not stated that submarines would be used in to sink merchant ships in an unrestricted submarine war, the fact that submarine design was altered proved that the capability for independent submarine operations was important. In 1920 the Navy was already considering using submarines to interrupt enemy lines of communication. It should also be noted that the Board was willing to reduce speed to increase endurance, which means, while not stated, unrestricted submarine war against merchants was as important as, if not more important than, submarines operating with the fleet.

The second issue before the Board in 1920 was a series of hearings with Electric Boat, one of the primary civilian submarine contractors, on the reliability of their proprietary Nelseco submarine diesel engines in the S-class. The debates were one of the catalysts for the Navy's decision to take full control of the submarine design process. It is important to understand how the Navy bought submarines at the turn of the century. Prior to 1917, the Navy relied on private industry to design submarines. This resulted in

---

[69]Ibid., 166.

[70]Ibid., 176.

self serving companies hording technology instead of making the best possible warships.[71] During the interwar period the Navy, through the Board, took control of the design process. Submarine expert Gary Weir observed that "The decision of the Navy Department to become deeply involved in submarine construction as a coordinator and catalyst proved one of its most profitable and significant policies of the 1914-1940 period." As the senior advising body in the Navy, the Board influenced the shift to Navy controlled designs.

The Board's hearings on the diesel problems were the first in a series of hearings the Board would hold on the S-class reliability. Every test of the S-class diesels resulted in failures of clutches, crankshafts and connecting rods.[72] The Navy's Bureau of Engineering (BuEng) requested that no S-class submarines undergo sea trials until corrections were made to the diesel engines. Electric Boat requested a hearing on the matter.[73] BuEng laid out a good case of the multiple problems with the S-class diesel, including reading an operating log that indicated 22 problems in a month and a half period that put the diesel engine out of commission.[74] Electric Boat acknowledged the problems, specifying torsional vibration and defects in the steel they acquired, and requested the contract be changed to allow operation at a lower engine revolution per minute (RPM) where vibrations did not occur. The lower RPM reduced engine power.[75]

---

[71]Weir, *Building American Submarines 1914-1940,* 2.

[72]Ibid., 92.

[73]GBH November 4, 1920, HBGB, roll 3, year 1920, page 936.

[74]Ibid., 961.

[75]Ibid., 956.

BuEng had already allowed the S-class engine ratings to be lowered in 1919 and believed that the only way to correct the problems was with an engine redesign.[76] The Board sided with BuEng's recommendations.[77]

Electric Boat continued to avoid complying, instead recommending minor changes to the engine at cost to the Navy, rather than a complete redesign.[78] The Secretary of the Navy took the Board and BuEng recommendation and forced Electric Boat to comply with the contract by withholding money. The resulting standoff between Electric Boat and the Navy resulted in a halting of S boat production until early in 1922.[79] The Navy was eventually willing to compromise with Electric Boat because it was in the Navy's interest to keep Electric Boat building submarines. Additionally, the Navy shared some of the responsibility since the S-class was a Navy design. The response of Electric Boat to the diesel problems furthered the Navy's belief that private industry, interested in bottom lines, should not control the submarine design process.

Captain Stirling's Letter

Captain Yates Stirling (see figure 8) was a submarine flotilla commander in WW I and future rear admiral. He had firsthand experience with the problems with U.S. submarines. As commander Submarine Flotilla of the Atlantic Fleet, two submarines that Stirling was on were almost lost at sea, due to a combination of inexperience and

---

[76]Weir, *Building American Submarines 1914-1940,* 93-94.

[77]Ibid., 95.

[78]Ibid.

[79]Ibid. 97.

unreliable equipment.[80] When Stirling reported only one of his six submarines qualified to dive in deep water, he was ordered to report his findings in detail. He sent a letter to the Secretary of the Navy, which was forwarded to the Board. The only submarine hearings before the Board in 1921 were on CAPT Stirling's letter. The hearings became an opportunity for submarine operators to voice their concerns.

Figure 8. RADM Yates Stirling
Source: Naval Historical Center, RADM Yates Stirling, http://www.navy.mil/navydata/cno/n87/images/sterling.jpg (accessed April 15, 2009).

CAPT Stirling's letter had been sent to numerous mid and senior grade submariners, including future admirals CAPT Hart and LCDR Charles **Lockwood,** to comment on the letter. Two main themes were discussed. The poor design and reliability of U.S. submarines, specifically the S-class and the inferiority of U.S. submarines compared to the German U-boats. Stirling agreed with BuEng's assessment

[80]Stirling, *Sea Duty: The Memoirs of a Fighting Admiral,* 155.

that the Electric Boat Nelseco diesel engines faults could not be corrected by beefing up components, but were instead due to a poor overall design.[81] One submariner, who added his comments for the Board, LCDR Percy Wright stated that "The engine situation in all our submarines, especially in the S-class is the most serious problem confronting the submarine service."[82] LCDR Sherwood Picking believed that "It would be criminal recklessness to attempt to handle the boat alongside a dock or tender on the [diesel] engines."[83] The general feeling among all respondents to the letter was that the U.S. should simply reverse engineer the German diesel engines and install them on all U.S. submarines.

The Navy acquired six German U-boats following WW I. They performed extensive testing and found them to be vastly superior to U.S. submarines. CAPT Stirling provided the Board with extensive testimony by officers who had tested the German submarines and all believed the German submarines to be superior. The characteristics in Table 1, which were provided to the Board, compare a German U-boat and an S-class submarine.[84]

---

[81]GBH June 30, 1921, HBGB, roll 4, year 1921, page 306.

[82]Ibid., 307.

[83]Ibid., 308.

[84]Ibid., 338-339.

Table 1. German U-boat compared to U.S. S-class		
	U.S. Submarine S-7	**German Submarine U-111**
Surface Speed	Normally 14 knots, reduced to 12.12 knots due to engines.	Normally 16.4 knots, actual 17.09 knots
Radius, Surface (endurance)	3967 nautical miles	3274 nautical miles
Time to Dive	2 min 30 sec	54 sec
Torpedo Tubes	4 bow tubes	4 bow and 2 stern tubes
Guns	1-4 inch	2-4.1 inch
Submerged Turning Diameter	613 feet	367 feet

Source: GBH, U-boat vs S-class (Washington, DC: HBGB, June 30, 1921), 338-339.

The Board would have had to note that in almost every category that the submariners believed important the German U-boat was superior. The S-7 was only better in endurance, but still did not have the radius necessary to operate in the vast Pacific Ocean, while the German U-boat could operate in the Atlantic Ocean. Captain Stirling stated that "It seems to me that U-111 was designed as a war boat with a clear view of necessary qualities. The S-boats were originally designed to win the bid over the Electric Boat Company proposal in competitive trials."[85] He continued by providing the following recommendation "My opinion is that in order to eventually build successful submarines it is first necessary to destroy the wrong principles and ideas which brought forth the S-boats. I had an opportunity to examine the plans of the V-boat and from this I

[85]Ibid., 339.

am led to believe that they will be no more successful than are our present submarines."[86] It was very clear to the Board that the U.S. submarine force thought the German submarine was superior to the U.S. submarine.

The problem of time to dive was discussed in depth by CAPT Stirling. Before nuclear power allowed submarines to stay submerged indefinitely, submarines had to be on the surface to recharge their batteries. When an airplane or another ship was seen the submarine would quickly dive and shift to operating with batteries and an electric motor, which meant the time it took for a submarine to submerge was important. When compared to the German U-boats, the U.S. submarines took much longer to dive. LCDR H. T. Smith believed "the most vital inherent fault in our submarines is their slow diving qualities, a factor applying directly to military value."[87] Most U.S. submarines took 1.5 to 5 minutes to dive; German U-boats could dive in under a minute in almost all cases.[88]

Stirling went so far as to recommend "that we don't continue to develop the S-class, but go to the German [submarine] and develop from there."[89] The submariners believed that the S-class unreliable design and poor quality along with the advances that were just being understood by reverse engineering the German submarines should compel the Navy to start over.[90] CAPT Hart was of the opinion that "our past methods of

---

[86]Ibid.

[87]Ibid., 316.

[88]Ibid., 317.

[89]Ibid., 336.

[90]Ibid., 337.

arriving at submarine design are considerably to blame for our long record of failures and that the situation seems unchanged."[91]

One portion of Stirling's testimony offered his additional views on how to design submarines. Stirling noted that "The submarine's principal weapon is surprise" and listed the elements of surprise as:

1. High surface speed, enabling a submarine to reach a good strategic or tactical position.
2. Quick diving qualities.
3. A most efficient listening device in order to detect surface or submerged vessels before the submarine can be sighted.
4. Long radius of action on surface and independence of outside repair facilities.
5. Weatherly qualities and good habitability, including ventilation.
6. Large radius submerged, in time more than distance.[92]

The list Stirling provided was based on experience, insightful and provided the Board many of the qualities needed for submarines in War Plan Orange.

1917-1922 Conclusions

While the Board understood Stirling's complaints, they did not agree that production of the S-class should be stopped. Instead, blaming engine problems on Electric Boat, they called for the Navy's Bureaus to become more involved with Electric Boat to solve the problem diesel reliability issues and incorporate German engineering.[93] It is to the Board's credit that they listened to Stirling and other submariners' firsthand accounts of problems, but did not abandon the need for a long range submarine capable

---

[91]Ibid., 336.

[92] Ibid., 333-334. He did not list high submerged speed. In fact said that an attack using high submerged speed resulted in a chance at being counter detected by the enemy.

[93]Weir, *Building American Submarines 1914-1940,* 37.

of independent operations that incorporated many of the qualities Stirling recommended. It would have been easy for the Board to recommend an exact copy of the German submarine, but that would have likely led a submarine suited to the Atlantic instead of the submarine that was needed for War Plan Orange, the *Gato* class.

CHAPTER 3

1922-1932

There was a belief in the Navy that bigger was better when it came to guns. Submarine deck guns were no exception. Treaties had limited the maximum size of submarine deck guns to 8 inches. Former Commander-in-Chief of the Asiatic Fleet Admiral Charles B. McVay believed that since "We are limited to 8-inch guns. I don't see why we should wait for somebody else to use them."[1] The Board discussed the problems with putting a bigger gun on the current submarine designs. The bigger gun puts "The center of gravity above the center of buoyancy" making the submarine unstable. To counter the additional weight, ballast would have to be put in the bottom of the submarine, significantly increasing the displacement and decreasing surface speed and endurance.[2] While not as big a concern, the drag caused by a bigger deck gun also reduced submerged speed. The Board did not recommend increasing deck gun size, instead choosing speed and endurance as priorities.

The 1922 discussion about deck gun sizes shows one of the problems with the Board transcripts. The obvious discussion that should have accompanied the technical feasibility of increased deck gun size was the tactical necessity of a bigger gun. The transcripts indicated that occasionally, the Board discussed some matters off the record. The necessity for bigger deck guns was one such issue. When Admiral Joseph Strauss asked if the reason for bigger deck guns was that the Navy was "preparing for a gun duel

---

[1]GBH October 23, 1922, HBGB, roll 5, year 1922, page 735.

[2]Ibid.

between submarines," the transcripts indicated that Admiral William V. Pratt responded "not for the record."[3] While there is no way to know exactly what was discussed, it was assumed that any perceived advantage of bigger deck guns was not worth the loss in speed and endurance.

Treaties and Budgets

In the 1920s, two issues had a significant impact on U.S. Navy construction and subsequently submarine construction. First, following WW I a treaty was signed that limited the size and composition of navies. Second, after military spending increased throughout WW I, Congress and the President cut military budgets. The result was that very few submarines were built in the 1920s and early 1930s.

The Washington Conference of 1921-1922, brought together the U.S., Great Britain, Japan, France and Italy to discuss naval arms limitations. The Washington Naval Treaty, or Five-Power Treaty, set limitations on total capital ship and aircraft carrier tonnage; individual ship size; maximum gun size; and included Article XIX which prevented countries from building or improving specified fortifications or naval bases in the Western and Central Pacific. Besides reducing the size of the Navy, the Five-Power Treaty froze U.S. capital ship construction and forced the Navy and the Board to concentrate on naval aviation, smaller surface combatants, support ships and submarines.[4]

---

[3]Ibid., 736.

[4]Kuehn, *The Influence of Naval Arms Limitation on U.S. Naval Innovation During the Interwar Period, 1921-1937*, 292.

Article XIX of the Five-Power Treaty had a unique impact on submarine design and strategy. Since the Navy was not allowed to build new bases or improve certain existing bases, submarines had to have large cruising radius to be effective in the vast expanse of the Pacific.[5] The Board was very aware of the restrictions of the Five-Power Treaty and its strategic implications for the Navy. In fact, the next submarine planned by the Board following the signing of the Five-Power Treaty gave up speed for endurance.[6]

In 1920 Republicans were elected to both the House and Senate. There was a significant buildup of the military for WW I and the new Congress limited military, and thus Navy, spending as part of President Harding's return to normalcy and the public's expectation of a peace dividend. During a time of general economic prosperity in the country, the Navy's budgets of the 1920's were relatively small.[7] Additionally, arms control treaties were easy to get ratified by a Republican Congress and Executive Branch looking for anyway to reduce the military's budget and increase international stability.

The impact of both the Washington treaty and the Republican Congress on submarine building was significant. From 1922 to 1932 only six submarines were built.[8] All six were V-class submarines. For comparison, from 1912-1922, 132 submarines were built and from 1932-1942, 127 submarines were built.[9] The limited opportunities to

---

[5]Ibid., 289-290.

[6]Friedman, *U.S. Submarines Through 1945*, 292.

[7]Kuehn, *The Influence of Naval Arms Limitation on U.S. Naval Innovation During the Interwar Period, 1921-1937*, 300.

[8]Friedman, *U.S. Submarines Through 1945*, 292.

[9]Ibid., 286-304. Statistics show the number of keels laid down, indicating that build money had been allocated by Congress and the Navy.

build submarines meant that the Board had to ensure that good design decisions were made. While it would seem to follow that a reduction in money to build submarines and treaty limitations would cause the Board to be less innovative, the opposite was often true. Limited fiscal resources and treaty constraints forced the Board to develop innovative and unique solutions to continue the advancement of submarine design. While all the 1920s submarine design decisions were not complete successes, they provided valuable lessons in submarine construction that would significantly benefit the Navy when the economic and geopolitical factors changed in the 1930s.

The *V-4*

Like any group that was examining future military systems, the Board debated and recommended submarine design features that would have limited value once built. Two such capabilities were examined in 1923. The first, submarine minelaying, was not a new idea. The first submarine, David Bushnell's 1775 Turtle, unsuccessfully attempted to place mines on British warships.[10] A submarine could place a minefield submerged in an unsuspecting enemy port or across their projected line of advance. U.S. submarines successfully mined Japanese ports in WW II using torpedo tube launched mines, but in the 1920s mines could not be launched from the same tubes as the torpedoes. The Board's 1923 design was a submarine primarily built for minelaying. A secondary capability of the 1923 design was a submarine launched sea plane. In theory, it was a great concept. A submarine could surface, launch a small scout plane that could search

[10]Friedman, *U.S. Submarines Through 1945*, 11-12.

for and even engage enemy targets. Unfortunately, it required a small quickly built plane and a large dry compartment on the submarine neither of which existed.[11]

The Board set the characteristics for only one submarine in 1923, the *V-4* (*Argonaut*), a unique boat that was the largest submarine the U.S. built until nuclear submarines in the cold war.[12] The primary mission of *V-4* (see figure 9) was long distance stealth minelaying with a secondary mission as a scout.[13] The *V-4* was slower, but had a larger range than the earlier V-class boats. Giving up speed for endurance was something the Board recognized had to occur for War Plan Orange. The Board felt that there was a historical case for minelaying submarines. In WW I, the Germans had success with submarine laid mines.[14] Even though submarines could not carry a large number of mines, the element of surprise made the mine fields very effective. The other unique mission of the *V-4* was as an extended range reconnaissance platform. The submarine's planned airplane gave the submarine an over the horizon detection capability before radar existed.

---

[11]GBH April 2, 1923, HBGB, roll 5, year 1923, page 96.

[12]Friedman, *U.S. Submarines Through 1945*, 290-292.

[13]Ibid., 176.

[14]GBH July 9, 1924, HBGB, roll 5, year 1924, page 293.

Figure 9. V-4
Source: Naval Historical Center, *V-4*, http://www.history.navy.mil/photos/images/h54000/h54425.jpg (accessed April 15, 2009).

Was the Board trying to make the *V-4* a do everything submarine? The Navy's budget had been cut following WW-I and the Board could only count on limited shipbuilding funds. If the Board could only build one submarine every couple of years, there would have been a temptation to try to put all the latest technology and concepts to continue advancing submarine design. The Board's transcripts on the *V-4* indicate they were trying to make a submarine that could do everything. For example, the Board envisioned the *V-4* would "lie in the enemy's trade routes and interfere with them for long periods."[15] This is a great mission statement for the successful WW-II *Gato* class, but difficult to accomplish on a submarine that has removed a significant number of

[15]Ibid., 294.

torpedoes and replaced them with mines, minelaying equipment and an airplane tank. Later, submarines were very successful multi mission platforms, but in the 1920's technology and submarine construction did not allow for incorporation of all the Board's desires. The Board also wanted something conceptual built that they could experiment with to test designs and concepts in the fleet. Building limited or single types of platforms was not necessarily something they wanted to avoid.

The Board's design of the *V-4* was ultimately a failure. The submarine launched seaplane was scrapped by the Board after difficulties were encountered designing a dry storage tank and an airplane that could be quickly assembled. To lay mines, the *V-4* used an advanced and problematic system to quickly lay mines and maintain submerged stability.[16] The system was a complex design that did not work as planned. The *V-4* ended up being heavy, underpowered, unreliable, and the last minelaying specific submarine the Navy would field. *V-4* never laid mines during WW-II and was converted to a troop carrier. Rear Admiral Richard "Dick" O'Kane, considered by many to be the most famous U.S. WW II submariners, reflected about his the time he spent on *V-4* early in his career. "*Argonaut* was a monster, a continuous challenge, with 12 torpedoes forward, 78 mines aft, and mounting two 6-inch guns that could hurl hundred-pound projectiles nearly 20 miles."[17] In an early WW II war patrol he noted that "half her major

[16]Friedman, *U.S. Submarines Through 1945*, 176. As mines are launched , weight leaves the submarine. The V-4 used numberous hydraulic motors to move mines and compensate buyoncy. With the V-4's large displacement, there was little room left for mines

[17]Richard O'Kane, *Clear the Bridge* (Novato, CA: Presidio Press, 1977), 16.

machinery became inoperative, but that did not stop Argonaut from carrying out her mission."[18] The *V-4* remained in service into WW II and was sunk by Japan in 1943.[19]

The Board continued to push the operational fleet and the Bureaus for better habitability. Most of the submariners that came before the Board were quick to point out that habitability was not a problem on U.S. submarines; however the reality was different. Reflecting back on his time on *V-4* RADM O'Kane stated "*Argonaut's* lack of air conditioning coupled with our required all-day dives resulted in ever increasing humidity and attendant electrical grounds, and fighting the ensuing small fires became almost routine."[20] Submariners thought they were tough enough to not let it bother them, but living in excessively hot and humid conditions reduced a submarines ability to carry out the mission. Eventually, the Board realized that unique stresses that submarines created and pressed for better conditions to improve submarine crew performance.

The *V-4* had a specified 18,000 mile cruising radius and was "designed with special reference to maintaining the health and comfort of the personnel for a period of 90 days."[21] Admiral William L. Rodgers asked "The story we heard from the Germans was that after 45 days on the cruising subs, they were pretty nearly ready to go to the mad house. Are we giving sufficiently improved quarters to avoid that?"[22] The submarine commander responding to the Admiral assured him that the submarine crew was up to the

---

[18]Ibid.

[19]John D Alden, *The Fleet Submarine in the U.S. Navy* (Annapolis, MD: Naval Institute Press, 1979), 29.

[20]Richard O'Kane, *Clear the Bridge,* 16.

[21]GBH April 2, 1923, HBGB, roll 5, year 1923, page 82-83.

[22]Ibid., 92.

task. ADM Rodgers continued to stress the Board's desire for improved habitability until he was convinced the design was acceptable. The Board had a unique ability to determine what design aspects were really important and press the designers to achieve the best results. The Board's primary product was a list of ship specifications, but since many of the designers were repeatedly called before the Board and, as senior leaders in the Navy, the Board could impact careers; the Board was able to ensure their wishes appeared in the built submarines.

V-5 and *V-6*

The Germans had a large (2000 ton displacement) submarine in WW I that traveled long distances at slower than fleet speeds.[23] The Navy saw the need for a similar design for War Plan Orange. While the WW I era Board was more interested in submarines that could operate at fleet speed, characteristics for a cruiser submarine were included in the 1919 Navy Department annual report.[24] While initial cruiser designs were not built, the idea stayed alive and the Five-Power Treaty Article XIX reinforced the need for a submarine that could deploy from Hawaii.[25]

---

[23]Friedman, *U.S. Submarines Through 1945*, 166.

[24]Ibid.

[25]Ibid., 170.

Photo # NH 45666 USS Nautilus (SS-168) during the early 1930s

Figure 10. *V-6*

Source: Naval Historical Center, *V-6*, http://www.history.navy.mil/photos/images/h45000/h45666.jpg (accessed April 15, 2009).

In 1925, the Board debated two submarines for following year's authorization, the *V-5 (Narwhal)* and *V-6 (Nautilus)*. The concept was for a submarine cruiser similar to the successful long range WW I German designs. Many in the Navy wanted a dual minelaying /scout submarine with more torpedo tubes than the *V-4*.[26] However, initial design studies yielded too heavy a submarine. In previous discussions the Board continued to put new capabilities on the *V-4* and by 1925 the Board recognized that a submarine with too many missions becomes less effective.

[26]Friedman, *U.S. Submarines Through 1945*, 179.

ADMIRAL HILARY P. JONES: Well, if you remember, we went through this argument and the object of the General Board has been right all along to get a combination boat—a minelaying and torpedo offensive as well—but we have run up against every time the question of combination that would give us the same speed and practically the same offensive qualities.

ADMIRAL HENRY A. WILEY: Well isn't that always the case, Admiral? When you try to make something do two jobs, you usually do not get satisfactory results.

ADMIRAL DAVID W. TAYLOR: It seems to me, to get a six million dollar boat to carry 60 mines, which could only make one trip a month across the Pacific – it strikes me as being pretty poor economy.

ADMIRAL JOSEPH STRAUSS: The Germans didn't hesitate to send one across the Atlantic and do up a cruiser and bump a hole in one of our battleships.

ADMIRAL TAYLOR: Well, you could do just as well with only one or two. It is pretty expensive to carry on a program of minelaying across the Pacific by using submarines.[27]

The Board realized that minelaying submarines were neither cost effective nor a strategic necessity. The Navy did not build a mine specific submarine after *V-4* and instead BuOrd developed torpedo tube launched mines.

Initial plans were for *V-5* and *V-6* to carry an airplane. Yet in 1925, the Navy still did not have an acceptable airplane designed. After seeing design plans, the Board realized that the plane's only value was as an observation platform.[28] Any plane launched from a submarine had to be so small that it could not carry any offensive armament. The question became -- was an aircraft whose assembly put the submarine at risk, provided no attack capability, and added a large tank to the submarine worth the extended observation range?[29] The plane did not exist in 1925, but it was "the opinion of

[27]GBH November 10, 1925, HBGB, roll 7, year 1925, page 504-505.

[28]GBH May 4, 1925, HBGB, roll 7, year 1925, page 262.

[29]Ibid., 272-274.

the War Plans Division that anything which can add to the power of observation is advantageous from the operational point of view."[30] Plans for an airplane were canceled on *V-5* and *V-6*, but based on the belief that an effective airplane would be built, the Board continued plans for an airplane on the last three V-class boats.[31]

The *V-5* and *V-6* served through WW II. Although both were considered unwieldy, each completed multiple war patrols, sinking 13 enemy ships. As more capable submarines came on line, *V-5* and *V-6* were shifted to covert troop and equipment transport. *V-6* was retrofitted to carry 20,000 gallons of aviation gas for long range refueling of seaplanes. Both submarines were decommissioned before the end of the war.

By 1925, the *V-1* had been in the fleet for less than a year. *V-2*, *V-3* and *V-4* were still in construction. Before the fleet submarine program that was initially started in 1919 had a chance to be evaluated, the Navy had shifted to larger and more expensive cruiser submarines. One aspect of submarine design missing from the Board's discussions is that of propulsion. Following the yet to be resolved problems of the S-class diesel problems, the Board had to be apprehensive about the reliability of the heavier V-class boats' engines.

---

[30]Ibid., 273.

[31]Ibid., 263.

Fleet Feedback on S and V-class Problems

In 1926 the Submarine Officer Conference (SOC) was established to provide a submariner's perspective to the General Board.[32] Since the submarine force was such a young branch of the Navy, no submariners had achieved the rank of Admiral, subsequently, immediately after WW I there were no Admirals on the Board that had any experience with submarines. The lack of direct submarine experience can be seen in some of the post WW I Board's submarine decisions. In hindsight the Board's push for fleet speeds in WW I era submarines was destined to fail. The technology simply did not exist to reliably propel a submarine that fast. Looking back, ADM Galantin noted that the early V class boats were bigger and faster, but the Board fell into the shipbuilding design flaw of "More horsepower meant more weight and space, more displacement, more fuel, more drag, more spare parts, more men, more cost, and so on."[33] The SOC was started to provide more submarine expertise to the Board. Instead of building submarines to achieve fleet speed the SOC lobbied for more endurance and better habitability.[34] The SOC eventually became very influential in the Board's decisions. By the mid 1930s the SOC's recommendations were often rubber stamped making the SOC like a subcommittee of the Board.[35] As Admirals, specifically RADM Hart, with more

---

[32]Brayton Harris. *Submarines: A Political, Social And Military History*. (New York. Berkley Books. 1997) 256.

[33]Ignatius J Galantin. *Submarine Admiral: From Battlewagons to Ballistic Missiles.* (Urbana: University of Illinois Press, 1995) 29.

[34]Ibid.

[35]There are many examples in the 1930s were the Board asked for or were presented the SOC's recommendation and the Board chose the SOC position with little debate.

experience in submarines became members of the Board, the SOC lost some influence, but remained an important advisory group through WW II.

War Plan Orange and the Five Powers Treaty demanded a long range submarine capable of traveling the 7,000 nm roundtrip from Hawaii to Japanese waters to conduct a war patrol. The maximum range of the S-class was about 6,000 nm, which limited its value in War Plan Orange.[36] In 1926 the Board discussed either modifying S-class to extend its range or building a submarine tender ship to accompany and refuel the boats.[37] A fuel tender would extend the range of three S-class boats to 18,000 nm and modifications to a single S-class boat would extend the range to 10,000 nm.[38] The fuel tender was a more expensive idea, which presented a problem to the other boats it was supporting if it was lost at sea so it was never built.[39] Experts warned the Board that any changes to the theoretical S-class maximum endurance would be lessened by the S-class habitability. The war plans division told the Board that S-class habitability was "such that they could not operate efficiently for more than 30 days."[40] Some changes were made to the S-class submarines in the interwar period, but none produced significant improvement in actual endurance.

The limited range of the S-class limited it to costal defense in War Plan Orange. The S-class would not be able to conduct offensive operations against Japan until the

---

[36]Friedman, *U.S. Submarines Through 1945*, 308.

[37]GBH April 11, 1926, HBGB, roll 7, year 1926, page 313.

[38]Ibid., 313-314.

[39]Friedman, *U.S. Submarines Through 1945*, 139.

[40] GBH April 11, 1926, HBGB, roll 7, year 1926, page 325.

U.S. seized forward operating bases. The V-class was the remaining contribution to War Plan Orange in 1926, unfortunately there were only three and initial feedback on the design was not favorable.

The V-class had three boats in the fleet or in sea trials and submariners had the chance to evaluate the performance. In 1927, a submarine division commander's letter was read before the Board detailing the problems:

1. Actual surface speed was 18 kts. The contract specified 21 kts.
2. Poor sea keeping qualities.
3. The diesel engine air intakes took in water in heavy seas or when water washed across the deck. Every time this happened, the diesel engines had to be stopped and dried. The result was that the submarine could only be operated in smooth water.
4. Diesel engine failures at certain engine speeds.
5. Fuel oil leaks.
6. Poor living conditions such that the reenlistment rates were unusually low and transfer requests were significantly high.[41]

Based on the letter, the War Plans Division told the Board that the V-class would not be able to fulfill the cruiser submarine requirements of War Plan Orange.[42]

Experts told the Board that because of the S-class limitations and the V-class problems, the submarine force was not ready for "war purpose".[43] Lack of speed and

[41]GBH April 1, 1927, HBGB, roll 7, year 1927, page 71-72.

[42]Ibid., 70.

endurance were common to all U.S. submarines and dominated the 1927 Board submarine discussions.

Speed was needed not only to keep up with the battle fleet, but also to position the submarine to attack enemy ships. The S-class could make 14 kts with a clean hull, but speed quickly dropped with even minor hull fouling.[44] Years of S boat operations had proven that sustained speeds above 10 kts resulted in propulsion machinery failures that could prevent the submarine from moving at all.[45] The result was the S-class could not achieve speeds above 10 kts for any length of time. The V-class problems kept them from operating in anything but smooth water on their diesel engines. In rough seas their battery powered auxiliary engines, which only propelled the V boats at 10 kts, had to be used.[46] The submarine force's effective speed of 10 kts would neither allow fleet action nor let submarines operate independently.

Perhaps a bigger problem for the U.S. submarine force was the submarine's poor endurance. Practical data showed that the S boats could operate 2,000 nm from a friendly base and while little data existed it was estimated the V boats could operate 3,000nm from a submarine base.[47] Habitability not considered, other issues were reducing submarine endurance. First, there was no way to tell how much fuel submarines had remaining. To keep the submarines buoyancy constant as it changed depths, the diesel

---

[43]Ibid., 77.

[44]Ibid., 75. Fouling was caused by sea growth attaching to a ship's hull. It makes the smooth hull less hydrodynamic, which has the effect of reducing speed.

[45]GBH April 1, 1927, HBGB, roll 7, year 1927, page 75.

[46]Ibid.

[47]Ibid., 76.

fuel tanks were filled with seawater as diesel fuel was used. The diesel and water would not mix and the fuel tanks were always full of a fuel water mixture. The operators, however, could not determine how much was fuel and how much was water. Additionally, to add seawater fuel tanks had an opening to the sea. As the submarine dove, the hull compressed and some fuel and water mixture would be lost through the opening, further complicating fuel estimates. Since fuel levels were unknown, commanders had to constantly limit their range to ensure they did not run out of gas.[48] Second, lubricating oil usage was higher than predicted. Submarines only carried a set amount of lubricating oil, which could also limit a submarine's endurance.[49]

Another problem with the V boats was their build time. V-class submarines took about three years to build.[50] If war came, the Board wanted a submarine that could be built quickly. The Navy had bad experiences with private shipyards prior to and during WW I. Navy experts called before the Board often saw private yards as more interested in making money rather than making a good submarine. Rear Admiral George H. Rock of the Bureau of Construction and Repair called the previous experience with private yards as "highly undesirable."[51] To better control the submarine building programs, all but one of the V-class was built at government shipyards.[52]

---

[48]Ibid.

[49]Ibid., 77.

[50]Ibid., 89.

[51]Ibid., 90.

[52]Weir, *Building American Submarines 1914-1940*, 41; 72-73.

The state of the submarine force in 1927 was poor and demanded a course change in submarine design policy. The V-class had started as a submarine capable of fleet speeds, and then shifted to a slower long range cruiser submarine. The V-class was bigger and more expensive than previous U.S. submarines. Budget constraints limited the numbers of V-class boats and due to design changes, as the class progressed, the boats were significantly different. With a limited number of ships numerous problems were created. Replacement parts were tough to obtain, since each boat contained many one of a kind parts. Sailors had to learn new equipment each time they transferred to a different submarine. Since each submarine design operated differently, lessons learned were not easily passed to other boats. Small ships like submarines were very expensive to build on a dollar per ton basis. To correct the problems the Board needed a cheaper and standardized submarine that could use economies of scale to further reduce price and increase effectiveness.

A New Direction

To build the next generation submarine the Board first looked to the successful German U-boats. The U.S. had already been copying and refitting S boats with German diesel engines.[53] The Bureau of Construction and Repair believed a 1,500 ton, 12,000 nm, and 12 kt submarine that was a copy of the German WW I U-135 should be the next design.[54] Unfortunately, almost ten years after WW I, the Board was still considering using a WW I design as the basis for the next submarine. Additionally, the Bureau of

[53]GBH April 1, 1927, HBGB, roll 7, year 1927, page 78.

[54]Ibid., 84.

Construction and Repair estimated that it would take five to six years before a copy could be built.[55] The challenge would be incorporating 10 years of submarine design lessons and the capabilities to accomplish War Plan Orange requirements.

Rear Admiral Frank Schofield, director of the War Plans Division (and a former member of the General Board), presented the Board with design specifications for a submarine that was very similar to the German WW I cruiser submarines. Specifically, RADM Schofield recommended a submarine that not exceed 1,600 tons and have:

1. Sustained surface speed of 12 to 14 knots.
2. Maximum speed of 15 to 17 knots.
3. Six torpedo tubes.
4. One 5-inch deck gun.
5. Cruising radius of 12,000 nm.
6. Habitability of 90 days.[56]

RADM Schofield was concerned that the aging U.S. submarine fleet would need to be replaced and the slow build rate would leave the U.S. with a small ineffective submarine force.[57] War plans no longer necessitated a high speed submarine, largely because attempts to build one had been unsuccessful. "Nothing in our experience has indicated that fleet submarines, so called, can render adequate return, for the money expended, in tactical cooperation with the fleet."[58] The Board's charter was now clear; they were no

---

[55]Ibid., 87.

[56]GBH December 1, 1927, HBGB, roll 7, year 1927, page 138.

[57]Ibid., 139.

[58]Ibid.

longer trying to make a submarine capable of fleet speeds, but a quickly built submarine capable of independent operations in the Pacific.

A smaller 1,500 ton submarine meant that some of the Board's design choices had to change. The submarine launched airplane added too much weight, size and complexity to be a viable option. Additionally, tests on the submarine launched plane showed that, while a good concept, it negatively impacted the submarines operations without providing significant advantage.[59]

The Navy's natural choice for more and bigger guns had to be reexamined. Rear Admiral William D. Leahy summed it up when he stated, "Guns are heavy. The weight of the 6-inch gun is 39,800 pounds; 5-inch, 24,000 pounds, in round numbers; 4-inch, 10,000 pounds, and the 3-inch is 5,400 pounds."[60] The multiple 5 and 6-inch guns of the earlier V-class were no longer an option. All the remaining boats after *V-6* built through the *Gato* class had only one gun that was less than 4-inches.[61] Limiting weight of deck guns became a much bigger concern when designing smaller submarines.

Correcting the Diesel Problems

Diesel engines continued to plague the submarine force in the late 1920s. The Board realized that submarines without reliable machinery would not benefit the Navy and most of the submarines in the fleet did not have reliable diesels. Immediately after WW I, there was a general feeling by the Board that a reliable diesel engine would be built and the Board did not need to get involved in the details on engine manufacturing

[59]Ibid., 167-168.

[60]Ibid., 177.

[61]Friedman, *U.S. Submarines Through 1945*, 309-311.

and construction. Unfortunately, diesels never became more reliable. By 1928, the Board realized that they had to become more involved to develop the diesel needed to power the submarines required by War Plan Orange.[62]

It is necessary to understand the history of diesel engine manufacturing to understand why the U.S. could not produce reliable diesel engines, when other countries could. The first submarine engines were gasoline engines, which proved to be dangerous in the confined spaces of a submarine. Since diesel fuel was less volatile, it was the next logical engine. However, diesel engines operated at higher pressures and temperatures leading to a more complex design. One problem was that no other U.S. industry used a diesel that met the unique challenges of operating on a submarine. Where a surface ship has almost unlimited room to house a diesel engine, submarines had a confined space, but had to retain much of the power requirements.[63] One of the reasons the post WW I Navy was interested in steam propulsion was that diesels could not be made that would provide the necessary power.[64] A smaller and more compact diesel had smaller parts that, unless fabricated correctly, were more prone to failure and the compact design was harder for mechanics to repair.[65]

When the U.S. examined captured German U-boats it became obvious that the German diesels were better designed and more advanced than any U.S. engines. The Navy copied German diesels and put them into some S-class boats with less success than

---

[62]GBH May 9, 1928, HBGB, roll 7, year 1928, page 146.

[63]Friedman, *U.S. Submarines Through 1945*, 256. A 1914 surface ship diesel weight to horsepower ratio was about 350 lb/BHP, while a submarine was about 60 lb/BHP.

[64]Ibid., 255.

[65]Ibid., 255-256.

the Germans achieved, but generally acceptable results.[66] Unfortunately, the German copies were not powerful enough to drive the large submarines required for War Plan Orange and U.S fabrication was not as good as German.

Destructive vibrations called torsional vibrations were caused when the submarine's diesel engines coupled directly to the propeller shaft operated at certain critical speeds that produced destructive shaking. This meant that at certain engine speeds the diesel engine would develop vibrations that would eventually cause the engine to fail. While all diesels were susceptible, torsional vibrations became a significant problem when the diesel was directly coupled to the propeller shaft because the diesel needed to operate at different speed, including the critical speeds, to change the submarine's speed. Larger diesels used on the larger submarines only worsened the problem.

In 1928 BuEng proposed to the Board using electric motors, which would not have torsional vibration problems, to provide propulsion. Separate diesel engines would be used to recharge batteries and provide electricity to the electric motors, which would in turn drive the propeller shaft. Unlike a diesel engine which provides varying torque to the propeller shaft, an electric motor provides near constant torque and does not experience torsional vibration. The problem was that the diesel electric configuration had not been attempted before and no engines existed.[67]

Previous machinery arrangements in submarines had the diesel engines connected either directly or through gearing to the shaft that turned the propeller. The diesels could

---

[66]Ibid., 259.

[67]GBH May 9, 1928, HBGB, roll 7, year 1928, page 146.

only be operated when the submarine was on the surface.[68] The submarine's batteries were either charged by the diesel that turned the propeller shaft or by a separate smaller diesel. When submerged, the submarine would operate on batteries that powered an electrical motor. In the late 1920s, the Board was presented with the idea of using a diesel electric arrangement to solve the submarine force's propulsion reliability problems. Diesel electric had multiple diesels that only produced electrical power that powered the electrical motor that turned the propeller shaft, charged the battery, or both. Submerged, diesel electric operated with the battery providing power to the electrical motor that turned the propeller shaft, similar to how all pre cold war submarines operated submerged.

Diesel electric offered a few big advantages over directly connected diesels. Since there were multiple diesel engines that did not have to be operated whenever the shaft was spinning, one diesel could be operated while another was secured for maintenance. Diesel electric was operated at a single speed that was most efficient and did not produce torsional vibrations. BuEng head Rear Admiral Samuel Robinson summed up the advantages:

> There are a great many advantages to the all-electric type of propulsion. We get away from the fact that submarines are now limited in the number of speeds at which they can run on account of critical speeds. This limitation will not apply not apply with electric propulsion. There will be no critical speeds. All engines can be used for both charging and propulsion and there are a great many other advantages besides. But the prime advantage is that we can get more horse power and a more reliable engine in the same space than we have in the past.[69]

---

[68]Until a snorkel mast was developed in the mid 1940s, submarines had to be surfaced to run their diesel engines.

[69]GBH May 26, 1933, HBGB, roll 9, year 1933, page 67.

There were some technological challenges to overcome to make diesel electric a reality. First, in 1928 diesel electric did not exist as the sole source of propulsion.[70] Second, with diesel electric, the electrical motor was always running and had to propel the submarine at higher speeds than a motor that was only used when the submarine was submerged. Finally, using 1930 diesels would have led to heavier machinery than direct coupled diesels, thus diesels with a better horse power to weight ratio had to be developed.

In a 1929 Board meeting attended by the SECNAV and the CNO, Rear Admiral Harry E. Yarnell, the Chief of the Bureau of Engineering, presented a study on diesel electric engines that had been requested by the Board. He concluded that:

1. There was not a diesel engine in existence that was acceptable.
2. There was no commercial application that would use a similar diesel engine, which meant that the cost of development would be high.
3. Because an engine did not exist, the diesel electric engines should be put in old S boats as a test prior to installation in new submarines.[71]

While RADM Yarnell (see figure 11) did not provide a glowing recommendation for diesel electric engines, the possibility of reliable submarine propulsion made building diesel electric prototypes a necessity. Many of the Board members were skeptical about the prospects of a diesel-electric submarine and agreed with RADM Yarnell that the

[70]Friedman, *U.S. Submarines Through 1945*, 249. Diesel electric was used in earlier submarines, by using the battery charging diesel to directly power the electric motor attached to the shaft. However it was only designed to propel the submarine at slow speeds and for limited periods of time.

[71]GBH May 9, 1928, HBGB, roll 7, year 1928, page 192.

diesel electric engines should not be installed on the remaining V-class boats, but rather be retrofitted on S-class boats.[72]

Figure 11. RADM Harry E. Yarnell
Source: Naval Historical Center, RADM Harry E. Yarnell, http://www.history.navy.mil/photos/images/h78000/h78393.jpg (accessed April 15, 2009).

By 1928 BuEng convinced the Board of the merits of diesel electric propulsion. Some S-class boats tested the concept by running only their electric motors and with some alterations were successful. The only piece of equipment wanting to make diesel electric a reality was a high speed diesel, which did not exist and had no current

---

[72]GBH August 15, 1929, HBGB, roll 8, year 1929, page 195-207. Some Board members express their concern about the diesel electric arrangement throughout the hearings after RADM Yarnell makes his presentation.

commercial applications.[73] Under BuEng head, RADM Yarnell, the impetus for diesel electric grew, but a producer could not be found.

In 1932, the new head of BuEng, Rear Admiral Samuel Robinson brought together all U.S. engine makers to persuade them to start development of high speed diesel engines for use in diesel electric systems. Five companies entered competition for a Navy contract after they saw the potential profit in developing engines for the Navy and eventually to the commercial railroads.[74] Winton Engine Corporation, later General Motors, offered the best design. The following year Fairbanks Morse and Hooven, Owens, Rentschler (HOR) also offered viable engines.[75]

The contest was a success. By 1933, RADM Robinson stated before the Board that diesel electric propulsion was ready for installation on submarines and that tests showed that diesel electric "gives more reliability and at the same time more speed."[76] The diesel electric configuration was exclusively used by the U.S. until 1945 and gave the U.S. submarines an advantage with reliable propulsion that was perfect for an independent deploying submarine. Additionally, the diesel electric configuration could be produced much quicker than surface ship steam plants and was subsequently successfully placed on smaller WW II surface ships.[77] Diesel-electric engines were used on most of the WW II submarines and were very successful. Reflecting back to his WW

---

[73]Friedman, *U.S. Submarines Through 1945*, 259. Diesel electric could have been used in locomotives, but no companies were willint to risk money during the depression to develop them.

[74]Ibid., 261.

[75]Ibid., 263.

[76]GBH May 26, 1933, HBGB, roll 9, year 1933, page 66.

[77]Friedman, *U.S. Submarines Through 1945*, 259-263.

II submarine command, Admiral Galantin said that the "diesels were marvels of ruggedness and reliability. Pushed time and again in emergencies beyond their design limits, they made all else possible."[78] The Board deserves great credit for pushing forward with diesel-electric design. Years of directly coupled diesel engines had proven to be unreliable and produced a submarine fleet that was not effective for independent submarine operations in support of War Plan Orange, so some change was necessary, but a complete redesign was a risky undertaking. The result of the gamble was perhaps the most significant submarine development in the interwar period.

What role did the Board have in diesel electric development? Most historians give credit for making diesel electric a reality to BuEng heads RADM Yarnell and RADM Robinson.[79] The Board's contribution was less overt. The Board held many hearings on submarine diesel electric problems. Simply by elevating the issue to their level, the Board put pressure on BuEng to solve the problem. During the hearings where the Board specifically discussed diesel electric the members believed, although not unanimously, that it was the best solution to the submarine diesel propulsion problems.[80] BuEng deserves a great deal of credit for pushing the technology and selling the idea to commercial industry, but the Board's continuing pressure on BuEng was likely just as important in the development of a reliable solution for submarine propulsion.

---

[78]Galantin, *Submarine Admiral: From Battlewagons to Ballistic Missiles*, 122.

[79]Both Friedman and Weir indicate that the two BuEng heads were the primary proponent in the Navy for diesel electric.

[80]Some Board members were worried what would happen if the electrical system failed.

The Rest of the V-class and the London Treaty

Construction on the 7th boat in the V-Class started in 1930. *V-7* (*Dolphin*) was a one of a kind submarine that weighed about half of the previous three V boats.[81] The Board had received good reviews of captured German WW I submarines and realized that the earlier V boats were too large and complex to be quickly produced in time of war.[82] While not an exact copy of the German U-boats, *V-7* was the U.S. take on the German design. It was a size between the S-class and earlier V-class. V-7's size, weight, speed and endurance were almost identical to the successful WW II Gato class submarines. While some submarines between *V-7* and Gato would be smaller, *V-7*'s design shows that the Board had determined the right size for a submarine in War Plan Orange. *V-7* served through WW II. She made three unremarkable war patrols early in WW II and was made a training ship as more capable submarines came into the fleet. *V-7* was scrapped in 1945.[83]

While copying the German designs pushed the Navy towards smaller submarines, the 1930 London treaty made reducing submarine size a Board priority. The London Treaty set a limit on total submarine fleet tonnage. Most of the Board discussions in 1930 were based on designing a submarine with a weight that would maximize the number of submarines, while still retaining the capabilities necessary for War Plan Orange.

---

[81]Edward C Whitman, "The Navy's Variegated V-Class."

[82]GBH April 1, 1927, HBGB, roll 7, year 1927, page 84. This was one of many discussions about copying German submarine designs.

[83]Friedman, *U.S. Submarines Through 1945*, 187.

Admiral Day summed up the impact of the London treaty on the Navy's submarine building program. He stated that the treaty held the U.S. submarine force to "52,700 tons, of which we have seven V's and eleven S's which will not be of age by the end of the Treaty, leaving us 29,700 tons which we may build by the end of 1936."[84] While the numbers differed with the assumptions, most Board discussions on submarine design in 1930 had an analysis of how the future submarine's weight would fit into the London treaty. The question before the Board was now one of individual submarine size.

Board chairman Admiral Mark L. Bristol recommended building two classes of submarines, one smaller for costal defense and one larger for fleet and independent operations.[85] Using the Board's 29,700 tons, the Navy could build eleven 2,700 ton submarines like *V-4* through *V-6*, or twenty 1,500 ton submarines like *V-7*, or thirty-seven 800 ton submarines like the S-class, or a combination. Immediately the larger submarines were discounted. The Board had already moved towards smaller submarines with the thought that the early V-class were too big and complex for the capabilities they provided. A material division representative of the CNO's office pointed out that "as large as those submarines [early V-class] were, they still only had four torpedo tubes, the same number as the S boats."[86] Small S-class like submarines were considered, but they did not have the range to quickly and independently cross the Pacific Ocean, a capability that would be required to reinforce remote Pacific bases under the limited ship

[84]GBH July 15, 1930, HBGB, roll 8, year 1930, page 268.

[85]Ibid., 269.

[86]Ibid., 279.

environment of the London treaty.[87] Additionally, smaller submarines would not be able to go far enough from port to counter fleets using the rapidly expanding range of aircraft carrier launched airplanes.[88] This left the Board with a midsized submarine as the best way to maximize numbers while still retaining the capabilities required by War Plan Orange.

V-8 (*Cachalot*) and *V-9* (*Cuttlefish*) were the last two V-class submarines, which completed the fleet boat building program that was authorized by Congress in 1916. Construction on *V-8* and *V-9* began in 1931.[89] The two submarines were the smallest of the V-class continuing the reduction in V-class size started on *V-7* and reinforced by the London treaty's requirements. *V-9* was built by Electric Boat, ending 10 years of the Navy's exclusive use of government shipyards.[90] Many innovations were put into *V-9* (see figure 9), including being the first submarine with a partial welded vice riveted hull, and a torpedo data computer that revolutionized torpedo fire control.[91]

---

[87]Ibid. The example given to the Board was moving boats from the canal zone to Honolulu, something the S-class could not reliably accomplish without some risk.

[88]Ibid., 292.

[89]Ibid.

[90]Ibid.

[91]Edward C Whitman, "The Navy's Variegated V-Class."

Photo # NH 77108 USS Cuttlefish in port, during the mid-1930s

Figure 12. *V-9*
Source: Naval Historical Center, *V-9*, http://www.history.navy.mil/photos/images/h77000/h77108.jpg (accessed April 15, 2009).

V-8 and *V-9*, while innovative, were ultimately too small, which limited their speed, endurance, and weapon load.[92] *V-8* and *V-9* were built before diesel electric engines were put on submarines. Both used a German MAN built diesel that suffered from the same torsional vibration problems as U.S. built direct drive engines.[93] Like *V-7*, each participated in the early WW II action, but as more capable submarines entered the

---

[92]Ibid.

[93]Ibid.

fleet, *V-8* and *V-9* were shifted to training duties.[94] Both were decommissioned in 1945.[95]

The Board was warned about making *V-8* and *V-9* too small. The Navy Department held a series of conferences with former submariners in 1930. The findings were that "a vessel smaller than approximately 1,200 tons could not embody the necessary sea keeping qualities, radius, speed, endurance, habitability, and offensive power necessary for efficient offensive operation"[96] *V-8* and *V-9* weighed 1,100 tons, which was less than the 1,200 tons recommended by the Navy department submariners. With the London treaty constraining them, the Board, despite warnings, became too limiting with respect to size.

Future Submarines of 1930

In 1930, the Board received a copy of a letter from the Commanding Officer (CO) of *V-5* on his impressions of the boat during her shakedown cruise. The CO listed the boat's major deficiencies as poor ventilation, excessive heat and internal noise from auxiliary equipment.[97] Describing the heat and ventilation problems, the CO stated that:

> In cool climates the ventilation is good, in the Tropics, the heat inside the boat was almost unbearable for anything but short periods of time. Under the best Peace Time operating conditions; surface, hatches open, the temperature of the motor room was approximately 120° F. The average temperature of the Officer's

---

[94]Ibid.

[95]Friedman, *U.S. Submarines Through 1945*, 292.

[96]GBH September 22, 1930, HBGB, roll 8, year 1930, page 372.

[97]Ibid., 373.

> country and [the] remaining crew's living spaces 96-101° F. It was found that the supply ventilation motor and fan heated the outside air about 8° during delivery.[98]

In the past, when concerns about heat inside submarines were addressed by the Board, submariners and Bureaus often told the Board that, while the heat was an inconvenience, it did not adversely impact operations. ADM Bristol took a stand after hearing the CO's comments:

> What I have in mind is that you can't put into fighting craft all the comforts that we might desire and in addition to that we don't consider that we would always be in tropical waters. So we must make some sort of compromise and without some comment on temperatures it would seem as if we would consider them out of all question in a boat that we would require for naval purpose.[99]

When *V-9* was built, it included the first air conditioning unit on a submarine, greatly improving habitability and the crew's ability to tactically employ the submarine.

Another issue before the Board in 1930 was the question of the number of torpedo tubes. With the decision to concentrate on submarines below 1,500 tons, the Board realized that large deck guns would not be able to be placed on submarines, which made the submarine's only effective offensive weapon the torpedo. Many experts recommended the Board put six bow and two stern torpedoes on new submarines.[100] This gave submarines eight shots before they had to reload, significantly improving their offensive capabilities. While additional tubes slightly increased weight, it was a much better offensive capability then bigger deck guns or submarine launched planes.

Since WW I, submarines had were able to shoot torpedoes that would turn up to 90 degrees from the initial course using a gyro. Unfortunately, a gyro shot was difficult

---

[98]Ibid.

[99]Ibid., 380.

[100]GBH March 27, 1930, HBGB, roll 8, year 1930, page 74-87.

to execute since calculations had to be made for own ship and target course and speed. Additionally, it was difficult to communicate changes to the torpedomen and for the gyro setting on the torpedo to be changed.[101] Thus, gyro shots were not often used by the submarine force. In 1932, BuOrd began work on a torpedo data computer (TDC) that would assist in inputting gyro settings. The TDC kept track of own ship's course, own ship's speed and estimated target parameters to remotely set the torpedo gyro settings.[102] The TDC first appeared on the *Dolphin* (*V-7*) and would significantly enhance torpedo fire control since the CO could maneuver torpedoes instead of maneuvering the submarine.[103]

1922 – 1932 Conclusions

To judge the Board's impact on submarine design from 1922-1932 two questions should be examined. First, what was the success of the submarines built during the period? Second, what were the design advances that were initiated during the period?

The submarines designed during 1922-1932 were all part of the V-class, which consisted of five very different submarine types shown in figure 13. None of them were operationally successful. By that narrow measure alone, the Board did not positively impact submarine design. However, the Board deserves credit for experimenting with the V-class. If the Navy simply produced nine copies of *V-1*, the V-class still would not have been more successful. Had the war started in 1933, the submarine force would not have

---

[101]Friedman, *U.S. Submarines Through 1945*, 195-196.

[102]Ibid., 196.

[103]The Board did not discuss development of the TDC prior to its initial development in 1933. However, they discussed the problems with setting gyros in many sessions with BuOrd present. Once the TDC was developed, the Board's specifications did include a TDC.

been ready, but for a war that started eight years later, the V-class experimentation provided submarines that gave the Navy numerous lessons to build upon. Considering that most of the submarines built after the V-class were successful, the Board's willingness to change the V-class design makes the V-class a necessary step and ultimately successful.[104]

Figure 13. V-class
Source: Naval Historical Center, V class beside USS Holland, http://www.history.navy.mil/photos/sh-usn/usnsh-c/ss170.htm. With seven submarines alongside, in San Diego harbor, California, 24 December 1934. The submarines are (from left to right): USS *Cachalot* (SS-170); USS *Dolphin* (SS-169); USS *Barracuda* (SS-163); USS *Bass* (SS-164); USS *Bonita* (SS-165); USS *Nautilus* (SS-168); and USS *Narwhal* (SS-167) (accessed April 15, 2009).

The second factor that should be examined is the implementation of programs and design features that would pay dividends for future submarines. First and foremost was the Navy and the Board's willingness to support diesel electric development. The

---

[104]Edward C Whitman, "The Navy's Variegated V-Class." Dr. Whitman argues that the V class was sucessful because of the experimentation that took place.

Board's continued pressure on BuEng to find a solution to submarine reliability problems, combined with the Board accepting progressive solutions to problems, led to the U.S. fielding the most reliable and advanced submarine propulsion through WW II. Advances like early torpedo fire control systems and air conditioning show the Board was constantly pushing for the best submarine designs available. Even examining ultimately failed technology, like submarine launched airplanes, illustrates the Board's desire to improve the fleet. Examining the design lessons learned with the V-class and the future programs started during the period, the Board positively impacted submarine design from 1922-1932.

CHAPTER 4

1933-1941

In 1930, the Board had been warned about making the last two V-boats too small. *Cachalot* (*V-8*) and *Cuttlefish* (*V-9*) weighed about 1,100 tons, which was less than the 1,200 tons recommended by Navy department submariners. By 1933, the Board was listening to hearings about the lack of space on submarines designed to the Board's specifications. The Bureaus of Construction and Engineering wrote a joint letter to the Board requesting a change to the characteristics of new submarines.[1] RADM Land, head of the Bureau of Construction and Repair, summed up the space inside *Cachalot*, "It is too tight quarters for reliability of operation, for reasonable habitability and primarily for the stowage of safety equipment that the Department requires them to carry."[2] RADM Land pointed out that "it is quite evident that to make overhauls, especially at sea, at any time, would be done under great difficulty and probably unsatisfactorily and ineffectively done."[3]

RADM Land believed that a 1,500 ton submarine was a much better size to meet the requirements of War Plan Orange.[4] The tonnage limitations of the London Treaty were now a bigger concern to the Board. A conversation between a Bureau of Construction Captain and Board chairman, Rear Admiral George R. Marvell, concerning

---

[1]GBH May 26, 1933, HBGB, roll 9, year 1933, page 64.

[2]Ibid.

[3]Ibid., 68.

[4]Ibid.

a small weight increase to get a 2 kt increase in surface speed showed the Board's belief that the Treaty allowances would change:

> CAPTAIN VAN KEUREN: How do we know that we are going to build up to the London Treaty before 1936? In the second place, how do we know what is going to happen in 1935 when we have another conference? It seems to me that we ought not give too much consideration to the loss of 170 tons per boat at this time when there is so much uncertainty about the whole subject.
>
> ADMIRAL MARVELL: That is true. Nobody knows what tomorrow may bring.[5]

Only three years after the Board believed its hands were tied by the London Treaty, submarine size was back up for debate.

Porpoise and *Perch*: The P-class

In June of 1933 the National Industrial Recovery Act (NIRA) was passed by congress as part of President Franklin D. Roosevelt's new deal. The Act included four submarines that would become the lead boats of the *Porpoise* class. Built to the Board's 1934 specifications, the *Porpoise* was a four ship class. In addition to making submarines larger, the Board made diesel electric engines standard on new submarines.[6] Weighing about 1,310 tons, the *Porpoise* class used four high speed diesels and three auxiliary diesel generators to power electric motors to turn the shaft and charge the battery.[7] Two of the boats were built by the government at Portsmouth using riveted construction and two were built by Electric Boat using stronger welded construction.[8]

---

[5]Ibid., 74.

[6]Friedman, *U.S. Submarines Through 1945*, 198.

[7]Ibid., 200.

[8]Ibid., 292.

The *Porpoise* showed the Board's willingness to increase submarine size, making up for their earlier mistakes, but while the *Porpoise* was bigger than the last two V-class, submariners still found the forward torpedo room too small for efficient reloading and maintenance.[9]

The Board's FY 1935 submarine characteristics became the *Perch* class which was similar to the *Porpoise* class and was sometimes considered part of the *Porpoise* class (see figure 14).[10] Consisting of six submarines, the *Perch* class used eight high speed diesels and two auxiliary diesel generators. The *Perch* class was the first class to make air conditioning standard.[11] Three of the Perch class submarines were built by Electric Boat and three by the government.[12]

---

[9]Ibid., 200.

[10]The Board and Friedman call the *Perch* a separate class, but other sources list it under the *Porpoise* class.

[11]Friedman, *U.S. Submarines Through 1945*, 200. Friedman refers to it as more dehumidification than air conditioning.

[12]Ibid., 292. Of the three built by the government, two were built by Portsmouth and one by Mare Island.

Photo # NH 49968 USS Porpoise near New London, Conn., circa 1936

Figure 14. USS *Porpoise*
Source: Naval Historical Center, USS *Porpoise*, http://www.history.navy.mil/photos/images/h49000/h49968.jpg (accessed April 15, 2009).

The *Porpoise* and *Perch classes* or P-class maintained the same offensive armament as the last two V-boats. The P-class had four bow torpedo tubes and two stern torpedo tubes. They could carry 16 torpedoes and one 3 inch deck gun.[13] The class weighed half as much as some of the V-boats; but, with the exception of a smaller deck gun, carried a similar offensive armament. With more reliable diesels and combat multiplying auxiliary equipment, the Board's specifications for the multi ship per year build were a success.

[13]Ibid., 310.

The ten boat P-class consisted of some of the first submarines to see combat action against the Japanese in WW II.[14] The class operated successfully throughout WW II. Four P-class boats were lost to the enemy.[15] Using the lessons learned from the V-class, the P-class was considered to be the fleet submarine the Board set out to build following WW I. The P-class had an 11,000 nm endurance that would be standard on all fleet submarines produced until after WW II.[16] While the P-class had a maximum speed of 19 knots (about 2 kts less when charging the battery) and would not be able to operate consistently with the fleet, the P-class had the endurance and armament that allowed operations in the Pacific theater in support of War Plan Orange.

The P-class presented the Board with their first opportunity make a large number of submarines over a short period. In three years, there were more submarines built than there were in the previous 10 years. Incorporating the recommendations of submarine officers, the Board still built a boat that fit in the treaty restraints. The Board's insistence on BuEng correcting previous problems with propulsion finally paid off with the P-class. While the first generation diesel electric design did have problems, it proved the most reliable and advanced submarine propulsion system fielded in WW II. In judging the Board's impact on submarine design, the P-class could be seen as the turning point where capable submarines became the norm.

During the interwar period, sonar became significantly more advanced and made submarines more capable. A ship's propeller and machinery made discrete and

---

[14]Bagnasco, *Submarines of World War Two,* 222.

[15]Ibid.

[16]Friedman, *U.S. Submarines Through 1945*, 310-311.

broadband sound that traveled through the water and could be detected using passive sonar. Additionally, ships could emit their own sound or pings using active sonar. Primitive sonar had been used in submarine warfare during WW I, with limited success.[17] By the mid 1930s, more advanced sonar appeared on submarines. The JK/QC sonar used passive sonar (JK) to find and classify targets and active sonar (QC) to determine targets bearing and range.[18] By 1939, submarines could use sonar to accurately determine targeting date out to 6,000 yards.[19]

The impact of sonar was significant. While WW II era sonar never advanced to the stage where a submarine could attack a target without raising a periscope, receiving early warning and additional targeting data improved a submarine's offensive capabilities.[20] By the start of WW II most U.S. submarines had variations of 1930s sonar. The Board was actively involved in monitoring the development of sonar. Early in the interwar period, the Board was primarily interested in surface ship sonar to help counter the submarine threat, but as sonar became more capable and the Board began to understand the utility of sonar on submarines.

Salmon and Sargo Classes

In 1935 the Board met to determine the proposed characteristics for the next submarine class. Board member Rear Admiral John W. Greenslade considered the *Perch*

---

[17]Willem D Hackmann, *Seek and Strike: Sonar, Anti-Submarine Warfare and the Royal Navy 1914-54* (London: Stationery Office Books , 1984), 1-5.

[18]Weir, *Building American Submarines 1914-1940,* 74. Re-designated QCD.

[19]Ibid.

[20]Friedman, *U.S. Submarines Through 1945*, 197.

class a big advance in submarines. He summed up the evolution of the Board's thinking about submarines:

> We were driven into the larger types by an idea that submarines would have to operate tactically on the surface with the Fleet. It was surface tactical considerations that drove us to extremes in size of submarines. The results of all the work and study that I have been able to bring to bear show that if we are going to use submarines they have got to be used in coordination with the Fleet but not in direct tactical maneuver with the Fleet. In order to do that efficiently we have to deprive ourselves of a great many features, one of which is size itself; one principal advantage of submarines lies in keeping the size down. These boats – we want them seaworthy, habitable, rugged, and I should say we want them simple; but beyond that they must be kept down to the lowest possible limits in order that we may use the advantage of their principal feature, which is keeping out of sight of people above the surface.[21]

The pure diesel electric designs had achieved good results, but BuEng was looking to further improve submarine propulsion. Composite propulsion systems were not new to U.S. submarines, but had always been less than successful due to vibrations. RADM Samuel Robinson described an early envisioning of a new composite engine room in a 1935 letter to the Board:

> In this arrangement there are six engines identical in bore and stroke, and major component parts. Two of them drive generators and are the primary means for charging batteries. They are available for propulsion when employing the electric drive principle. The other four are arranged for a modified mechanical drive, two engines per shaft. Each pair of these engines connect to a common pinion of a reduction gear through fluid couplings commonly called Vulcan couplings.[22]

The composite propulsion system was lighter than the P-class diesel electric design, took up less space, and was more accessible for maintenance.[23] The Board agreed with BuEng's propulsion solution. The *Salmon* class (Board's FY 1936 characteristics) used

---

[21]GBH February 15, 1935, HBGB, roll 10, year 1935, page 30.

[22]Ibid., 38.

[23]Friedman, *U.S. Submarines Through 1945*, 203.

two diesels connected to the shaft through a hydraulic clutch and two diesel generators that provided power to electrical motors.[24]

Figure 15. USS *Salmon*
Source: Naval Historical Center, USS *Salmon*, http://www.history.navy.mil/photos/images/h69000/h69872.jpg (accessed April 15, 2009).

In addition to a new propulsion system the *Salmon* class had other unique features. The Board put four torpedo tubes forward and four tubes on the stern.[25] A

[24]Bagnasco, *Submarines of World War Two,* 223.

[25]GBH February 15, 1935, HBGB, roll 10, year 1935, page 31.

TDC fire control system was standard on the class.[26] The *Salmon* displaced 1,435 tons, about 100 tons more than the P-class.[27] The six boat class was of an all welded construction.[28]

Another important aspect of submarine endurance was submerged endurance. Unlike surface endurance, which increased as machinery reliability and fuel increased, submerged endurance was usually limited by battery capacity. The small S-class submarines could make 5 kts for 20 hours and the larger V-class boats could only make 5 kts for 10 hours. Both classes had batteries that contained between 8,500 and 9,500 amp-hours of energy.[29] A submarine on a war patrol would often remain submerged during daylight and surface at night to charge their battery. Therefore it was important to have a battery that could sustain the submarine through an entire day. The smaller S-class had the capability to stay submerged throughout the day, but as submarines became larger, their ability to stay submerged all day suffered.

Following the V-class, the Board increased the capacity of submarine batteries. By the time the *Salmon* class had been developed, battery capacity had increased to stay submerged for 48 hours at a slower speed of 2.5 kts.[30] *Salmon* had batteries that

---

[26]Ibid., 32.

[27]Friedman, *U.S. Submarines Through 1945*, 310.

[28]Ibid., 202.

[29]Ibid., 309-310.

[30]Ibid., 202.

contained 12,400 amp-hours of energy.[31] The rest of the fleet submarines, including *Gato* and *Balao*, had similar battery capacities and submerged endurance.

In 1936, once construction had started on composite power plant on the *Salmon* class, BuEng realized that the composite propulsion plant created some problems and requested to shift submarine propulsion back to an all diesel-electric design. While lighter and more compact, the composite power plant was more complex.[32] BuEng's request was not initially accepted by the Board. Rear Admiral Thomas C. Hart pointed out that "All electric drive is vulnerable in that flooded bilges under main motor, or generators, can completely disable the boat. And a similar result could follow one insulation or other electrical fire."[33] Eventually, the Board became convinced and the last submarines built in 1937 and all subsequent submarines were diesel electric.[34]

While surface speed was no longer the most important characteristic of submarines, it was still important. Following WW I the Board was very interested in developing a submarine that could consistently achieve greater than 21 kts to keep up with the battle fleet. Despite repeated specifications set by the Board, technology never advanced enough to produce a satisfactory propulsion system capable fleet speed. As submarine strategy evolved and treaty requirements shifted the Board to smaller submarines, surface speed became less important. Once diesel electric was proven successful, increasing surface speed again became a submarine force and Board priority.

---

[31]Friedman, *U.S. Submarines Through 1945*, 309-310.

[32]Ibid., 203.

[33]GBH February 15, 1935, HBGB, roll 10, year 1935, page 32.

[34]Friedman, *U.S. Submarines Through 1945*, 203.

Commander Charles A. Lockwood, the future Pacific submarine force commander, described his experiences with V-boats that led him to recommend higher surface speeds. Discussing a fleet exercise in which he was involved CDR Lockwood stated:

> I was on one of those ships, the *Cachalot* [*V-8*], and by making her force speed under her engineering limitations, which was about 14.7 knots, we did reach a position ahead of the fleet but in so doing we were unable to charge batteries. . . . All of these exercises have required high surface speed and usually with the fleet submarines we have now, it has been a difficult problem to get them there in time.[35]

While the impetus for increased speed continued to be the ability to operate with the fleet, faster surface speeds were also vital to repositioning to attack merchant ships. Standard steaming speed for most merchants was 12-13 kts, thus a speed faster was required for a submarine to reposition and attack. With the *Sargo* class, the Board set a requirement for submarines to achieve a sustained surface speed of 17 kts with one engine down for maintenance or charging the battery.[36]

The ten boat *Sargo* class was built to the Board's FY 1937 specifications and was very similar to the *Salmon*. The last five boats of the class returned to an all diesel electric design.[37] War loaded *Salmon* and *Sargo* classes could make about 17 kts on the surface while recharging their batteries.[38] Settling on exclusive diesel electric propulsion, the submarine force had a plant that was reliable over the large distance of the Pacific. While the new fleet boats still could not make the post WW I Board's specification of 21 kts needed to keep up with the battle fleet, they were fast enough for

---

[35]GBH October 15, 1937, HBGB, roll 11, year 1937, page 324.

[36] Friedman, *U.S. Submarines Through 1945,* 204.

[37]Ibid.

[38]Ibid., 203.

the independent operations required by War Plan Orange. The *Salmon* and *Sargo* classes were successful in WW II. They continued operations after the war and were all decommissioned by 1948.[39] The two classes were well received, showing that the Board had set the specifications for a boat that had consensus across the Navy.[40]

Tambor Class

In 1936, Rear Admiral Joseph K. Taussig, from the office of the CNO, stated to the Board that "the chief characteristics of any submarines which we may build shall be first reliability, second habitability, and third endurance… then we should put in all the offensive and defensive facilities that are practicable but not at the expense of any of those three primary ones."[41] It is interesting to see how the Navy's, and subsequently the Board's, priority for submarines had changed. While there was still some desire for submarines to operate with the fleet, the Navy was more interested in a submarine that could operate independent of fleet. About twenty years earlier the Board's primary characteristic for submarines was surface speed. The shift in thinking was most likely due to a maturing of the submarine force and Navy leadership that was impressionable during the German submarine operations in WW I. In 1936, the CNO's approved purpose for submarines was described: "Under the present accepted conception of submarine usage, they are to be employed for long radius open sea operations, and are intended to operate independently or with the fleet, but not as a 'Battle Task Force'."[42]

---

[39]Bagnasco, *Submarines of World War Two,* 223.

[40]Weir, *Building American Submarines 1914-1940,* 74.

[41]GBH March 8, 1936, HBGB, roll 10, year 1936, page 9.

[42]Ibid.

In 1937, fleet feedback on the *Porpoise* class was positive and construction was in progress on the *Salmon* class. Commander R. H. English, the senior member on the *Porpoise's* sea trials called the boat "far superior to anything we had on our smaller submarines like the S classes."[43] Submariners brought before the Board suggested some minor changes such as in increase in the number of torpedo tubes to six forward and two aft and continued enhancements in habitability.[44]

Figure 16. USS *Tautog*
Source: Naval Historical Center, USS *Tautog*, http://www.history.navy.mil/photos/images/h69000/h69872.jpg (accessed April 15, 2009).

---

[43]GBH March 4, 1937, HBGB, roll 10, year 1937, page 104.

[44]GBH March 8, 1936, HBGB, roll 10, year 1936, page 16-18.

In 1937, CDR Lockwood explained the importance of multiple bow and stern torpedo tubes:

> I believe that 60 per cent of those attacks are made with the bow tubes. However, with the fast zigzagging target the commanding officer can never tell definitely that he is going to attack with the bow tubes. Frequently at the last moment he is left with a situation in which he has to use the stern tubes. Therefore to have four tubes in the stern that is very important. Naturally, I would prefer to have six forward and four aft if possible.[45]

In a trend that became more regular throughout the 1930s, the Board followed the submarine force's recommendations; the Board gave the *Tambor* six bow torpedo tubes and four stern torpedo tubes. They could carry 24 torpedoes and one 3 inch deck gun.[46] The gun foundation was able to house a 5-inch gun because "we are committed not to use the submarine for economic warfare, but treaties seem to mean very little these days and we might someday be forced into that by our adversary and with an eye to the future it might be advisable to put on a 5-inch foundation for guns in order to be prepared for such an eventuality."[47] The added weight for the 5-inch foundation proved to be worthwhile. While submarines would have been foolish to get into a gun battle against frontline warships, the bigger deck guns proved valuable for engaging lightly armed auxiliary ships, especially early in the war when torpedoes were defective.

While the offensive capabilities of submarines had increased, there were still significant limits. CDR Lockwood described fleet torpedo firing exercises to the Board

---

[45]GBH October 15, 1937, HBGB, roll 11, year 1937, page 337.

[46]Friedman, *U.S. Submarines Through 1945*, 311.

[47]GBH October 15, 1937, HBGB, roll 11, year 1937, page 337. A CDR from BuNav to the Board.

to show how torpedo accuracy quickly decreased with range. In the exercise, four exercise torpedoes were fired at different ranges and the following data in Table 2 was collected.[48]

Table 2. Torpedo Test Data

Range	Hits	Misses
750 yards	4	0
900 yards	2	2
1200 yards	2	2
1800 yards	0	4

Source: GBH, *Torpedo Test Data* (Washington, DC: HBGB, 24 May 1938), 65.

CDR Lockwood summed up the results "I don't believe that with the small numbers of torpedoes we have, firing at ranges over 1000 or 1200 yards is justified."[49] The data also showed the importance of carrying the maximum number of torpedoes. The *Tambor* carried 24 torpedoes double the S-class's 12 torpedoes. The Board understood that a submarine that ran out of torpedoes lost most of its offensive capability and effectively reduced its endurance. By increasing the number of torpedoes submarines carried the Board improved submarines' impact in War Plan Orange and, probably unknowingly, created a hedge against the unexpected torpedo problems that occurred early in WW II.

CDR Lockwood's discussions with the Board in the late 1930s show how the U.S. submarine force had matured. CDR Lockwood's career was largely spent on and

---

[48]GBH May 24, 1938, HBGB, roll 11, year 1938, page 65.

[49]Ibid.

connected with submarines. In the 1920's the submariners called before the Board like Nimitz, Stirling and Yates usually only had one or two tours of duty on submarines. The submarine force now had Commanders and Captains who had spent their entire career in submarines providing the Board with recommendations. In fact, there was a noticeable decrease in the time the Board spent discussing submarine specifications from the early to the late 1930s. In hearings in 1937 multiple post command submariners provided the Board a number of recommendations. In the 1920's, officers that came before the Board to discuss submarines often only had one tour on submarines or were associated with submarines only on the periphery. The increase in the submarine force's influence on Board decision as the interwar period progressed was obvious.

In the later 1920s and early 1930s, the Submarine Officers Conference (SOC), the advisory group to the CNO on submarines and submarine related issues created in 1926, became more influential.[50] Throughout the 1930s, the Board deferred to the SOC on many matters involving submarines making the SOC a de facto sub-committee of the Board. The SOC gained more and more influence with the Board, to the point where it rubberstamped many submariner and SOC recommendations. Eventually, submarine admirals like Hart and Greenslade came to the Board and the submarine force's recommendations received senior level checks.[51] The importance of a more knowledgeable and mature submarine leadership providing input to and eventually becoming members of the Board cannot be understated.

---

[50]Ernest Andrade, "Submarine Policy in the United States Navy, 1919-1941" *Military Affairs*, 1971: 54.

[51]During two hearings in 1937 on submarines (presided over by RADM Hart) officers from the Submarine Officers Conference were before the Board answering more and harder questions about their recommendations than earlier in the decade.

The twelve submarine *Tambor* class was built according to the Board's FY 1939 specifications. Weighing about 1,475 tons, the *Tambor* class used four high speed diesels and two auxiliary diesel generators to power electric motors to turn the shaft and charge the battery.[52] They could make 18 kts on the surface while charging their batteries.[53] Only slightly less capable than the *Gato* class, the *Tambor* class was very successful in WW II. The USS *Tautog*, a *Tambor* class boat, sank 26 enemy vessels during the war, the most by any one submarine.[54]

Rear Admiral Hart and a Brief Return to Smaller Submarines

While other Board members had experience in submarines, arguable none had more experience than RADM Hart who arrived at the Board in the summer of 1936. RADM Hart had been involved with submarines since prior to WW I and had spoken before the Board throughout his career. By the start of 1937, he was Chairman of the Board. In 1937 RADM Hart presided over Board hearing on submarines. He provided a lengthy overview of the previous 15 years of submarine development because for him it was "difficult from what we had in our files to follow the various steps in development

52Friedman, *U.S. Submarines Through 1945*, 311.

53Friedman, *U.S. Submarines Through 1945*, 204

54Bagnasco, *Submarines of World War Two,* 224.

over the last few years."[55] The tone of RADM Hart's discussion was not always favorable to previous Board's decisions on the direction of submarines.[56]

In describing the impact of the SOC on the Board, RADM Hart stated "The General Board in all of its work in submarine characteristics has been very largely guided, for several years, by the Submarine Officers Conference of which all of us are cognizant; that Conference has been of greatest possible help."[57] With the arrival of RADM Hart to the Board,

SOC recommendations were no longer rubber stamped by the Board. Nowhere was RADM Hart's influence more obvious than the building of the *Mackerel* and *Marlin.*

RADM Hart wanted smaller costal submarines to replace the aging S-class submarines. In response to RADM Hart's desires the SOC said to Board "It was the unanimous opinion of the Submarine Officer's Conference that the requirements for submarines as approved by the Secretary of the Navy on 17 March 1936 will be better met by a 1,450 ton submarine of the *Sargo-Salmon* type. . . . The Conference further feels that it is not prepared to scrap several years of progressive work and study of the Submarine Officers Conference and respectfully adheres to its former opinion that the needs of the submarine service and the requirement of the Fleet are best met by a submarine of the *Salmon-Sargo* characteristics."[58] While the submarine force as a whole

---

[55]GBH March 4, 1937, HBGB, roll 10, year 1937, page 95. In addition to not being favorable to previous Board submarine hearings, the questions he asked were significantly more in depth than previous Board hearings.

[56]Ibid., 94-102.

[57]GBH October 15, 1937, HBGB, roll 11, year 1937, page 321.

[58]Weir, *Building American Submarines 1914-1940,* 45.

was split on the idea of small submarines, the advising group that had significantly influenced the later V-class and post V-class submarines was initially against them.

Figure 17. CAPT Hart
Source: Naval Historical Center, CAPT Hart, http://www.navy.mil/navydata/cno/n87/images/hart.jpg (accessed April 15, 2009).

When he joined the Board in 1936 RADM Hart ordered studies conducted on the feasibility of smaller submarines.[59] RADM Hart stated that, "It seems that the General Board never came anywhere near to deciding that we should use any of our limited displacement in purely defensive types, but the agreement was easily reached that we should build as *V8* and 9 the smallest boat which would answer general purposes. I don't find that those general purposes were ever very definitely agreed upon in this room or elsewhere, but the idea involved designing for long radius and protected sea

[59]Friedman, *U.S. Submarines Through 1945*, 221.

endurance."[60] RADM Hart argued for a return to "more moderate dimensions" that could be quickly produced and used for defensive costal operations.[61] Discussions before the Board showed that some submarine and Navy experts were for smaller submarines, but most were against the idea. The War Plans Division noted that "We do not have enough submarines of the larger type at the present time…and until we do get enough I think we ought to build large submarines to carry as many torpedoes as we can and be prepared to stay on station for as long a time as possible." [62] In the end RADM Hart used his position as Board chairman to have smaller submarines built. He even convinced the SOC who in 1938 recommended a submarine force structure of 44 larger fleet submarines and 30 small submarines.[63]

RADM Hart worked with L. Y. Spear of Electric Boat to design the smaller submarine.[64] The Board's characteristics for a small submarine were submitted in the summer of 1938.[65] From the Board's specifications two small submarines were built. The *Mackerel* was built by Electric Boat and the *Marlin* was built by Portsmouth.[66] The boats had a surfaced displacement of approximately 800 tons, a cruising radius of

---

[60]GBH March 4, 1937, HBGB, roll 10, year 1937, page 94.

[61]Friedman, *U.S. Submarines Through 1945*, 222.

[62]GBH May 24, 1938, HBGB, roll 11, year 1938, page 54. CDR Murphy explaining War Plans Division position on smaller submarines.

[63]Friedman, *U.S. Submarines Through 1945*, 227.

[64]Ibid., 223.

[65]Ibid., 224.

[66]Ibid., 227.

approximately 6,500 nm, two directly coupled diesels that made a surface speed of approximately 16 kts, and six torpedo tubes.[67]

Neither submarine was successful. Their range was not sufficient for War Plan Orange.[68] Larger fleet submarines could perform the smaller boat's mission, but the smaller boats could not be used as an independent deployer. Building the smaller submarines took a dry dock that could have been building a fleet submarine.[69] The *Mackerel* and *Marlin* were primarily used for training in WW II and were scrapped in 1946 and 1947.[70]

RADM Hart often takes a lot of criticism for using his influence to have the *Mackerel* and *Marlin* built, but there was little cost for the endeavor. The Board transcripts were very clear that no one, including RADM Hart, wanted to stop building larger fleet submarines. Building the *Mackerel* and *Marlin* did not prevent two fleet submarines from being built; instead the *Mackerel* and *Marlin* were built in addition to the FY fleet submarines. One of the big problems with the small submarines was that by the time they were built, the U.S. was mobilizing for WW II.[71] The two boat class did not fit into the U.S. war plans. Instead all shipyard resources went into producing fleet submarines. Perhaps if there were more small submarines by the time the war started, they would have been more successful. At the very least, the *Mackerel* and *Marlin*

---

[67]Ibid., 311.

[68]Bagnasco, *Submarines of World War Two,* 225.

[69]Friedman, *U.S. Submarines Through 1945*, 224.

[70]Bagnasco, *Submarines of World War Two,* 225.

[71]Friedman, *U.S. Submarines Through 1945*, 227.

confirmed the size of the fleet boats was the right size. RADM Hart's small submarines may not have positively impacted submarine designs, but if there was negative impact it was small. The real criticism of RADM Hart was that he used the Board's and his time on a project that in hindsight had little chance of success.

The Mark XIV Torpedo Problems

The Mark XIV (14) torpedo was designed in 1930 for the fleet submarines. It replaced the Mark X (10) torpedo, which was used on the S-class and had been in service since WW I. Unlike earlier torpedoes, the Mark 14 used the traditional contact exploder. Additionally, it had a new magnetic influence exploder to detonate the torpedo under a surface ship and break the ship in half.[72] The Board's involvement in developing the Mark 14 was limited to receiving updates on its progress. One update described the Mark 14 torpedo as"a much more reliable performer without loss of military characteristics."[73] Based on transcripts, the Board had little reason to think that the Mark 14 would be anything but a major leap forward.

The magnetic influence exploder was a big technological jump over previous contact exploders. To ensure the technology was not compromised the new exploder was developed in secrecy. The magnetic influence exploder was lab tested and limited tests occurred in the Atlantic Ocean, but a live fire test of the weapon was not conducted. The lack of testing and not aggressively finding and fixing the likely design flaws were a significant step back for the submarine force and the Pacific War effort.

---

[72]Blair, *Silent Victory,* 55.

[73]GBH May 24, 1938, HBGB, roll 11, year 1938, page 64.

Problems with the Mark 14 torpedo surfaced very early in WW II. In December of 1941, the captain of the *Sargo* had numerous well shot torpedoes fail to explode.[74] More and more captains discovered problems with the Mark 14 torpedoes. Reflecting back on his time as a WW II CO, ADM Galantin stated that "In what can only be described as a torpedo scandal, our submarines had been sent to war for 21 months with a defective weapon."[75] On then LCDR Galantin's first was patrol he shot 23 torpedoes, had only one hit with a normal explosion, and three others hit as duds.[76] BuOrd refused to acknowledge a problem existed.[77]

Figure 18. VADM Lockwood
Source: Naval Historical Center, VADM Lockwood, http://www.navy.mil/navydata/cno/n87/images/lockwood.jpg (accessed April 15, 2009).

---

[74]Blair, *Silent Victory,* 141.

[75]Galantin, *Submarine Admiral: From Battlewagons to Ballistic Missiles,* 90.

[76]Ibid., 88.

[77]Friedman, *U.S. Submarines Through 1945*, 243.

In June of 1942, six months into WW II, newly promoted RADM Lockwood ordered testing unauthorized by BuOrd on the Mark 14 torpedo that showed torpedoes operated about 10 feet deeper than they were set.[78] RADM Lockwood noted that dropping dummy torpedoes from a crane onto a steel plate resulted in all duds, showing that the contact exploder was also bad.[79] The Mark 14 torpedo suffered from four distinct problems that masked each other, which in a wartime environment made diagnosing and correcting the problem difficult. First, the Mark 14 usually operated 10 feet deeper than set, which caused the torpedo to go right under its targets. Second, the magnetic exploder sometimes prematurely fired, causing the weapon to explode before it reached the target. Third, sometimes the torpedo would circle back towards the firing submarine. Finally, the contact exploder usually failed to explode the warhead.[80]

RADM Lockwood ordered the exploders modified in Pearl Harbor and went to ADM Nimitz with the data and requested to send modified exploders on patrol. ADM Nimitz immediately concurred and on September 30, 1943 the *Barb* went on patrol with the modified exploder and reported no significant exploder problems. With the modified exploder RADM Lockwood recalls that the submarine force "made the Pacific a graveyard for enemy shipping."[81] He noted that the first four submarines to deploy with

---

[78]Blair, *Silent Victory,* 275.

[79]Lockwood, *Sink 'Em All*, 100.

[80]Douglas A Shireman, "U.S. Torpedo Troubles During World War II" *World War II Magazine,* (February 1998). http://www.historynet.com/us-torpedo-troubles-during-world-war-ii.htm/ (accessed February 22, 2009). "Veteran submariner and historian Paul Schratz said he 'was only one of many frustrated submariners who thought it a violation of New Mexico scenery to test the A-bomb at Alamagordo when the naval torpedo station was available."

[81]Lockwood, *Sink 'Em All*, 101.

the modified torpedoes reported greater than 50 percent hit rates and no duds.[82] The test and the fact that surface ship Mark 15 torpedoes were suffering similar faults ensured BuOrd acknowledged the first of many faults. Twenty-one months into WW II, most of the problems with the Mark 14 torpedo and its exploder had been corrected.[83] Once corrected, the Mark 14 proved to be a good weapon that performed as originally planned. Figures 19 and 20 show the improvement in torpedo performance after the exploder problems were realized and corrected.

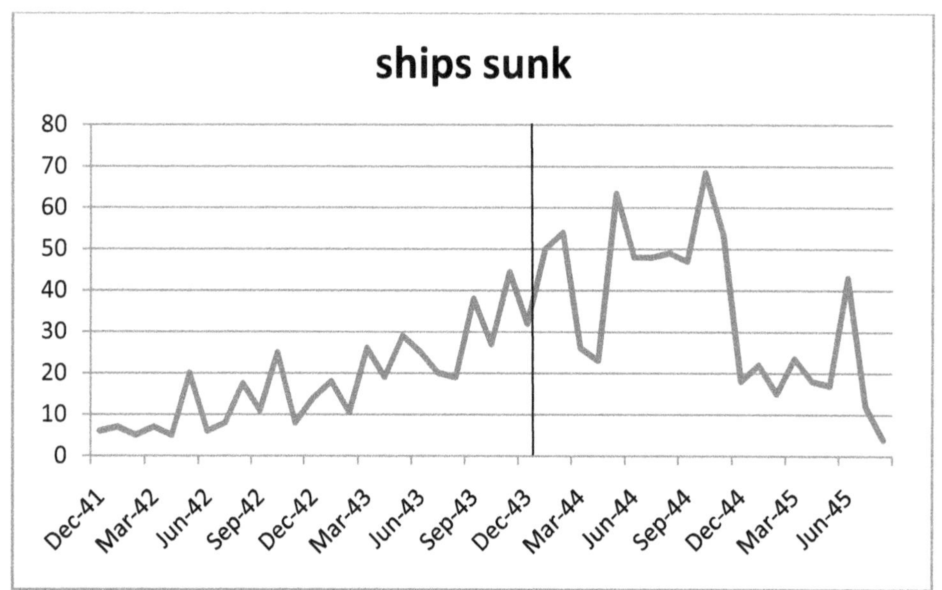

Figure 19. Ships Sunk by the U.S. Submarine Force in WW II.
Source: Data was compiled from multiple sources and then put into an excel spreadsheet to analyze.

---

[82]Ibid., 117.

[83]Blair, *Silent Victory,* 439.

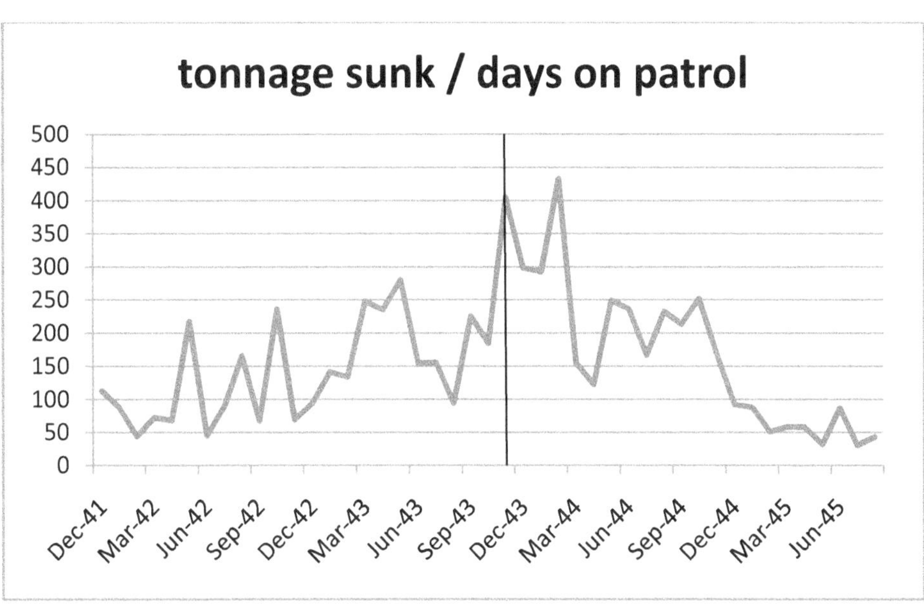

Figure 20. Normalized Tonnage Sunk by the U.S. Submarine Force in WW II. *Source*: Data was compiled from multiple sources and then put into an excel spreadsheet to analyze.

So who was at fault for the Mark 14 torpedo problems? Most historians place the blame on BuOrd.[84] Once problems began to surface with the Mark 14 torpedo, BuOrd was slow to investigate problems often placing the blame on the submarine crews for improper operation.[85] BuOrd notified S-boat commanders that their Mark 10 torpedo was running four feet deeper than designed and the problem was easily corrected. While many in the submarine fleet believed the Mark 14 torpedo suffered from a similar problem, BuOrd did not issue a similar warning.[86] BuOrd's handling of the Mark 14 problems has been called "derelict".[87]

---

[84]Robert Gannon, *Hellions of the Deep: The Development of American Torpedoes in World War II* (University Park, PA: Penn State Press, 1996), 202. Many other sources credit the failure to BuOrd.

[85]Blair, *Silent Victory,* 170.

[86]Ibid., 160.

[87]Ibid., 361.

Does the Board escape all blame? To answer this question, the Board's relationship with the Bureaus should be explored. Reading the transcripts leaves little doubt that while the Bureaus did not work for the Board they had to answer the Board's questions. Had the Board insisted on more testing, it is likely that more testing would have been done. Even with the Board pressure, the secrecy of the Mark 14 torpedo might have prevented live firing exercises in the Pacific prior to the war, but at least there would have been earlier indications that the torpedo was faulty.

The Board transcripts give no indication that the lack of testing on the Mark 14 was discussed before the Board, but members of the Board came from BuOrd, which certainly knew about the lack of testing, and the fleet, which likely knew about the lack of testing. More than likely the Board, at least some members, knew about the lack of testing of the Mark 14. The most that can be said about the Board's culpability was that they likely knew about the lack of testing, but had no reason believe the weapon would not work as designed. Since the historical evidence does not directly link the Board's decisions with the failure of the Mark 14, the Board was not directly responsible for the Mark 14 torpedo problems.

Arriving at the *Gato* class

In setting the initial 1942 building characteristics, which would become the *Gato* class, RADM Hart requested the Board vote on increasing the number of torpedo tubes to ten, with six forward and four aft.[88] With a vote of 10 to 6, personnel present at the hearing recommended ten tubes. A submariner from the CNO's office explained the

[88]GBH March 4, 1937, HBGB, roll 10, year 1937, page 114.

reason for additional tubes: "The time the torpedoes are needed for counter attack is just after the submarine has made an attack on some other type of ship. He hasn't the time to get his tubes reloaded for a counter attack and I think if he has torpedoes in the tubes, both forward and aft, he is in a much better position to protect himself."[89] Those against ten tubes believed the extra weight would not be worth the capability. In the end the Gato class was built with ten torpedo tubes, a decision that would serve the Navy well in the Pacific War.

The *Gato* class was built with one 3-inch deck gun, but the Board specified that the foundation be able to be refitted with a 5-inch gun. Submarine deck guns were much more effective in WW II than anticipated. The Japanese had many small auxiliary ships that were not worth wasting a torpedo. The deck gun allowed submarines to skink the smaller craft without wasting their valuable torpedoes and by the end of WW II the 5-inch gun was standard on submarines.[90] The Board had come full circle on gun size.

---

[89]Ibid., 115.

[90]Friedman, *U.S. Submarines Through 1945*, 214.

Photo # NH 50192 USS Wahoo off the Mare Island Navy Yard, 14 July 1943

Figure 21. *Gato* class USS *Wahoo*
Source: Naval Historical Center, *Gato* Class USS *Wahoo*, http://www.history.navy.mil/photos/images/h50000/h50192.jpg (accessed April 15, 2009).

Compared to the offensive capabilities of earlier submarines, the *Gato* was an impressive ship. With the evolution of sonar and the wartime development of radar, the Gato could find targets at a distance. The TDC quickly solved fire control problems allowing more torpedoes to find their mark. With 10 torpedo tubes and a deck gun, the Gato class was well adapted to the needs of War Plan Orange.

The *Gato* class weighed about 1,526 tons. Like the *Tambor* class, it used four high speed diesels and two auxiliary diesel generators to power electric motors to turn the shaft and charge the battery.[91] *Gato* could make 21 kts on the surface.[92] With the *Gato*

[91]Ibid., 311.

[92] Ibid.

class most of the problems with the high speed diesel-electric propulsion system had been corrected and the engine design remained the same to increase wartime production.[93] RADM Lockwood described the reliability of the diesel-electric design:

> *Tunny*, for instance, under pressure of war exigencies made a 1,200 mile run at full speed, averaging about 19 knots, without any sort of a casualty. To those of us who had grown up in submarines, where power plant breakdown were a matter of routine, with a resultant deplorable condition of engine room paint work, the spotless white-painted Fairbanks-Morse engineering spaces looked like paradise.[94]

The propulsion problems that plagued the submarine force for close to 20 years after WW I had finally been solved. The U.S. submarines Achilles heel, was now one of its strengths.

Depth charges were a significant danger to submarines. Usually dropped from surface ships, depth charges were explosives that could be set to detonate at a set depth. If they exploded close enough, the submarine would be damaged or destroyed. Navy testing in 1940 reveled that depth charges had to explode within 14 feet of a submarine to destroy the submarine by breaching the pressure hull, within 30 feet to damage the submarine and within 60 feet to significantly shake the submarine.[95] Besides remaining undetected, the submarines best defense was to be at a different depth than the depth charges were set. Increasing the maximum depth increased chance of a submarine surviving in a depth charge attack.

---

[93]Friedman, *U.S. Submarines Through 1945*, 206.

[94]Lockwood, *Sink 'Em All*, 371.

[95]Friedman, *U.S. Submarines Through 1945*, 205.

Test depth was the maximum depth a submarine could safely go to on a routine basis and the depth that the submarine was tested to during sea trials. With the exception of a few V-class submarines, the test depth of most submarines prior to the *Gato* class was 250 feet.[96] Submarines could operate deeper than test depth, and often did in WW II, but risked equipment failure as sea pressure increased. The Board understood that increasing the test depth of submarines improved their chances of diving under depth charges. A representative of the War Plans Division explained that:

> You will force three different depth settings on a 600-pound charge to cover the depth range, if you can go to 300 feet. This will cause the enemy to use more depth charges. If you can only go to 250 feet, two depth settings will cover the range. 300 feet also provides increased range, in depth, for escape and a stronger hull for resistance to depth charge attack at any depth. The second reason is that [Naval researchers have] been investigating strata in which listening gear is more or less ineffective. Those strata varied anywhere between 200 and 300 feet.[97]

The Board set the test depth for the *Gato* class at 300 feet and the subsequent *Balao* class at 400 feet.[98] In fact, the biggest difference between the *Gato* and *Balao* class were the hull material. The *Balao* class had a thicker hull.[99] Dick O'Kane took the *Balao* class *Tang* to more than 600 feet. The increased depth range significantly decreased effectiveness of depth charges, Japan's primary anti-submarine weapon, and saved many submarines from being destroyed.

Submariners had near unanimous praise for the *Gato* class. RADM Lockwood called the Gato class "the excellent all purpose submarine which had been designed for

---

[96]Ibid., 311.

[97]GBH November 9, 1939, HBGB, roll 11, year 1939, page 358.

[98]Friedman, *U.S. Submarines Through 1945*, 311.

[99]Brayton Harris, *Submarines: A Political, Social And Military History* (New York: Berkley Books, 1997), 261.

just the type of warfare that we were waging in the Pacific."[100] Dick O'Kane was transferred from *V-4* and became the Executive Officer (XO) of the *Gato* class *Wahoo* where he would team with Lieutenant Commander Dudley "Mush" Morton forming one of the most famous CO/XO combinations in U.S. submarine history. Reflecting on the differences between *V-4* and *Wahoo* RADM O'Kane stated, "Of half the displacement and with twice the power, *Wahoo* would have twice the *Argonaut's* speed and maneuverability. Further, she would carry 24 instead of 12 torpedoes and had ten instead of four tubes to launch them. To me, the living spaces seemed more like a streamlined train's than a submarine's."[101] O'Kane's *V-4* shipmate and CO of the *Gato* class *Halibut*, ADM Galantin, reflected that "combat operations had proved that the basic design of the fleet boat, although not thoroughly 'de-bugged' by war's start, was excellent for operations in the Pacific and permitted incremental improvements as combat urgencies prodded technologic progress."[102] With the help of Navy organizations like the SOC the Board had significantly contributed to the production of the reliable, habitable and powerful submarine required by War Plan Orange.

Conclusions 1933-1941

From 1933 to the start of WW II the Board continued to improve on the later V-class submarines. The *P*, *Salmon*, *Sargo*, and *Tambor* class submarines were all improvements over previous submarines. In fact, the P-class could be seen as the turning point where capable submarines became the norm. The diesel-electric design that the

---

[100]Lockwood, *Sink 'Em All*, 27.

[101]O'Kane, *Clear the Bridge,* 17.

[102]Galantin, *Submarine Admiral: From Battlewagons to Ballistic Missiles,* 122.

Board pushed in the late 1920s proved to be the best submarine propulsion system used in WW II.

The Board's impact on submarine design during 1933-1941 should really be judged by the *Gato* class submarines. The Gato was very well received by submariners. ADM Lockwood praised the *Gato* class and the people responsible:

> Due to conscientious work on the part of the Submarine Officers' Conference at the Navy Department, sympathetic and farsighted action by the General Board of the Navy and skillful design development on the part of the Bureau of Ships, we were able to start World War II with a standard type of Fleet submarine. This boat, with 10 tubes, 20 to 21 knots surface speed, long cruising radius and endurance, was built for just such work as was required in the Pacific. No major changes were made in it during the war.[103]

The *Gato* class was certainly not the perfect submarine. The Mark 14 torpedo was initially a failure, however with the information they had, there was very little the Board could have done to correct the problem. The *Gato* class could have been faster, had more endurance or been more habitable, but with the characteristics set by the Board, the Gato was the right submarine for War Plan Orange.

---

[103]Lockwood, *Sink 'Em All*, 369.

CHAPTER 5

CONCLUSIONS

As a group of men that set the specifications for submarines, the evidence strongly suggests that the Board had a positive influence on interwar submarine design. U.S. submarines made significant advances from WW I to WW II. While a certain level of advancement in two decades was to be expected, the U.S. went from a force that was unsuccessful operating close to the coast to one that was very successful operating in the great distances of the Pacific Ocean.

There were some Board actions that can be regarded as questionable. RADM Hart used his position as chairman to have two smaller submarines built. The SOC did most of the work on submarine design for the Board over about a ten year period. While not responsible for the early WW II failures, the Board should have had more oversight of the Mark 14 torpedo. However, none of Board decisions prevented the U.S from fielding a very capable submarine at the start of WW II.

A good way to view the Board was as a process and forum for the most influential submarine experts. Using this paradigm, there was no doubt that the Board was a success. The Board was a clearinghouse for ideas. While the Board had no legal powers within the Department of the Navy, they held the key to determining submarine design. Looking at the Board as a forum for ideas, a group like the SOC was not acting in place of the Board but rather as a part of the Board for the betterment of the submarine force. The Board seemed more than willing to augment itself as it saw fit to achieve certain ends.

Impact on Surface Speed, Endurance, Habitability and Offensive Armament,

While the thesis discussed many areas of submarine design and operations in the interwar period, the Board's decisions were primarily compared with the capabilities dictated by War Plan Orange using four factors. The first was speed; specifically surface speed, which allowed a submarine to quickly cross the Pacific Ocean to its patrol areas and position itself for an attack on enemy ships. The second was endurance which was a key aspect of being able to operate from U.S. bases in enemy water. The third was habitability which includes the air quality and crew comfort that was needed for long-range operations. Finally, submarine's armament was evaluated. This was primarily an examination of torpedoes and torpedo delivery systems. Deck guns, which were used with limited success in WW II, were investigated to a lesser degree. Each of these factors was examined in discrete time frames within the interwar period.

No one factor took up more of the Board's time than developing reliable propulsion that could maximize surface speed. Following WW I, the Board wanted a 21 kt steam driven submarine that could operate with the fleet. The Board's was presented evidence that a steam driven submarine was technologically infeasible and so they changed their position to continue using diesel propulsion, but did not abandon the fleet submarine. Figure 22 shows the maximum surface speed throughout the interwar period. The first V-Class submarines had maximum speeds around 21 kts, but they were so overweight and unreliable that they could not operate with the fleet or independently. Essentially the Board made *V-1* through *V-3* unreliable surface ships that could submerge instead of submarines. The Board overestimated U.S. diesel technology. The submarine diesel continued to be a problem throughout the 1920s.

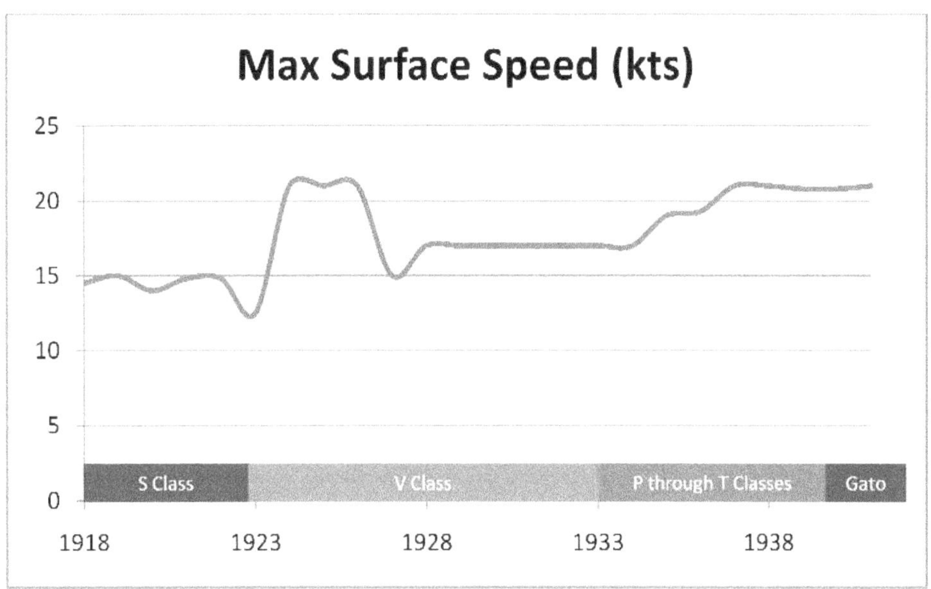

Figure 22. Maximum Surface Speed During the Interwar Period.
Source: Data was compiled from multiple sources and then put into an excel spreadsheet to analyze.

Eventually, the Board determined that maximum speed was not the most important characteristic. The Board argued that endurance and habitability were more important and they reduced surface speed specifications for the remainder of the V-class. While reliability improved on the later V-class, diesel problems still plagued the submarine force. The Board continued to call for improvements in submarine diesels eventually pushing BuEng to work with civilian industry to develop a reliable diesel electric. By the end of the interwar period the time the Board spent on submarine propulsion had paid off. The submarine force had a very reliable diesel-electric system that by the start of WW II could even reach and maintain the 21 kt surface speed initially sought by the Board. While WW II submarines rarely operated with the fleet, the reliable diesel-electric engines served the Navy well. The Board made a positive contribution to improving surface speed in the interwar period.

Endurance and habitability were examined together because of their symbiotic relationship. Throughout the interwar period, the Board pressed the operational fleet and the Bureaus for better habitability knowing that the crew's physical and mental conditions were directly related to the submarine's endurance. The Board was better than the submarine force leadership at realizing the unique stresses that submarines created. For operations in the tropics, the lack of air conditioning was a real drain on the crew. The Board made special effort to ensure air conditioning was placed on submarines. Machinery endurance was largely a benefactor of the time the Board spent on solving the diesel problem. Once diesel-electric propulsion was standard on submarines, endurance was significantly enhanced simply because machinery problems were less likely to force a submarine back to port. The Board made a positive contribution to improving habitability and endurance in the interwar period.

By increasing the number of torpedoes submarines carried the Board improved submarines' impact in War Plan Orange. Figure 23 shows the number of torpedo tubes throughout the interwar period. The Board continued to put more torpedo tubes on submarines. For a submarine operating independently, often attacking multiple targets, additional torpedo tubes were the difference between being sunk and surviving the encounter. It was interesting to note that the heaviest interwar submarine was *V-4*, which only had four torpedo tubes. Weighing half as much as *V-4*, the *Gato* had 10 tubes. The Navy and Board deserve credit for giving the submarines that fought WW II more than twice as much torpedo firepower without reloading as earlier submarines.

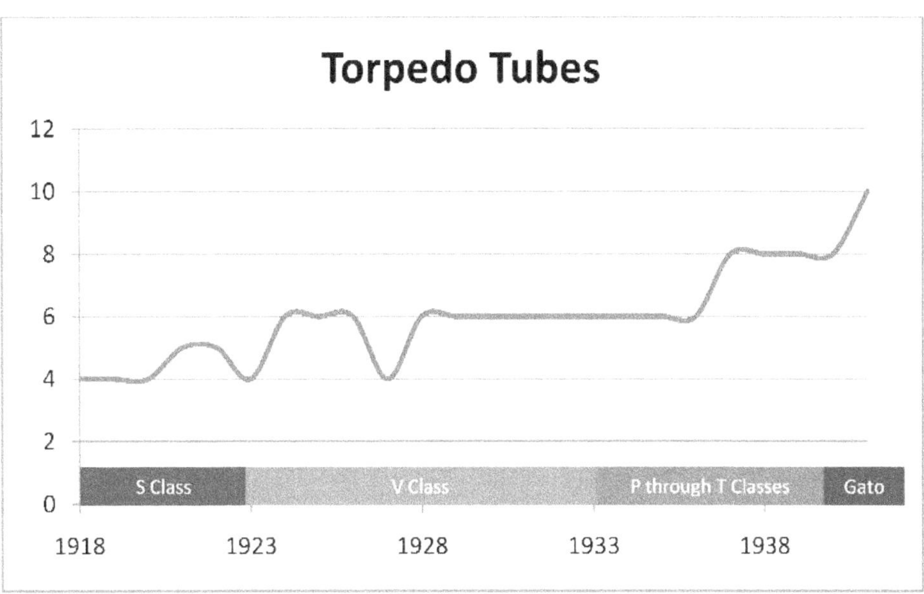

Figure 23. Number of Torpedo Tubes During the Interwar Period.
Source: Data was compiled from multiple sources and then put into an excel spreadsheet to analyze.

Instead of sticking with Navy tradition and providing submarines with the biggest deck guns possible, most submarines entering WW II had only 3-inch deck guns. The Board had put 6-inch guns on some of the V-class, but as submarine size decreased, so did the size of deck guns. Even though the prevailing thought prior to WW II was that submarines would never get into a deck gun battle, the Board put a deck gun foundation on the *Gato* class that could support a 5-inch gun. The decision proved to be a good one since many small Japanese auxiliary ships were not worth a torpedo and would be difficult to sink with just a 3-inch gun.

The Board had a positive impact on surface speed, endurance, habitability and offensive Armament. The improvement in all areas was significant. The Board's decisions and the processes the Board oversaw were directly responsible for most of the advances.

Other Observations

While not one of the factors that this thesis examined, surface displacement provided unique insight into interwar submarine development. Surface displacement was a good indicator for submarine size. Figure 24 shows surface displacement during the interwar period. Note the rise in size from the S-class to *V-4*, which was the heaviest submarine until after WW II. Treaty obligations, greater construction times and increased complexity led the Board to significantly reduce the size of the last two V-class submarines. The Board was warned about making *V-8* and *V-9* too small and despite warnings, became too limiting with respect to size. Even with the reduction in size, the 1,100 tons of the *V-7* and *V-8* was much closer to the 1,500 tons of the *Gato* class than it was to the 3,000 ton *V-4*. The gradual rise in surface displacement was largely due to the Board making minor modifications to submarines after the V-class. Additional features like torpedo tubes, sonar equipment, TDCs and air conditioning all added small amounts of weight that greatly increased the effectiveness of submarines.

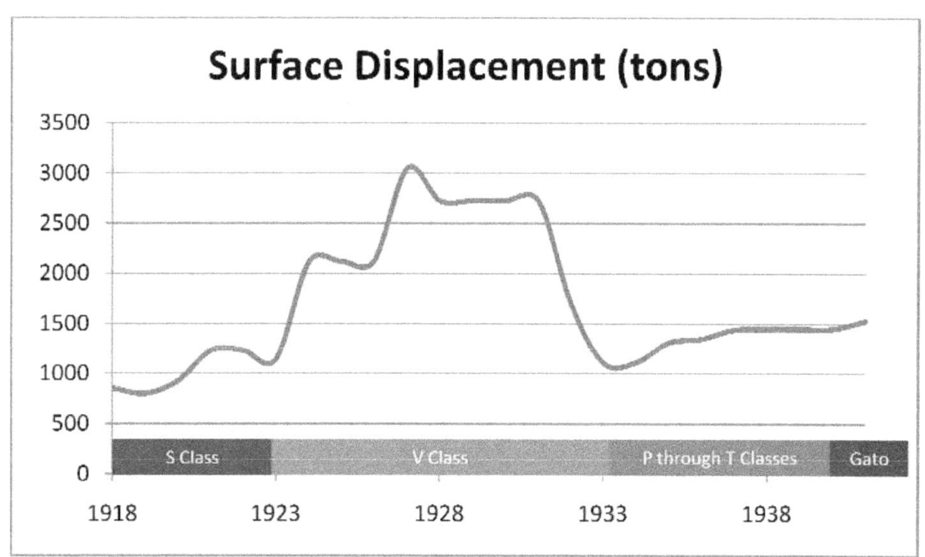

Figure 24. Surface Displacement During the Interwar Period.
Source: Data was compiled from multiple sources and then analyzed.

The Board had the ability to bring the most relevant experts together to make informed decisions. The Board received firsthand accounts of submarines operations getting the most up to date and relevant information and intelligence on a topic by bringing together the best submariners of the day and allowing them to directly influence design decisions. The Board had a unique ability to determine what design aspects were really important and press the designers to achieve the best results. Since many of the designers were repeatedly called before the Board and, as senior leaders in the Navy, the Board could impact careers; the Board was able to ensure their wishes appeared in the built submarines.

During the interwar period, submarine experience on the Board increased. Upon the advent of the interwar period, the submarine force had only been in existence a very short time compared to the surface force. There were no admirals on the Board that had any extensive experience dealing with submarines during the early interwar period. The lack of experience could be seen in the hearings by the number of questions asked to clarify general submarine operations and design. As the submarine force matured, the Board started to get admirals that had served on or around submarines. By the time RADM Hart became chairman of the Board, there was significant submarine knowledge on the Board and the Board's questions became much more specific and pointed. The maturation of the Board's submarine expertise certainly aided in designing a better submarine.

While the Board concentrated on ship design, they often discussed Navy policy and strategy. The Board discussed using submarines to disrupt sea lines of communication in a possible war against Japan as early as 1920. The War Plans Division was at most Board discussion on submarines. The Board's discussions likely made their way to the CNO's office and influenced strategy.[1] Because of the depth of Navy material discussed by the Board, the Board transcripts are a great source for understanding the high level discussions that shaped submarine design decisions. The transcripts were very detailed and were a great primary source for research. The transcripts contained the reasoning behind almost all design choices in addition to good insight into strategy, policy and relationships in the Navy.

Areas for Continued Analysis and Research

The problems with the Mark 14 torpedo hurt the U.S. war efforts and cost many sailors' lives. This thesis concluded that the Board had little opportunity to prevent the issues with the Mark 14 torpedo and exploder. This conclusion was reached after a review of the Board transcripts and secondary literature. Because of the magnitude of the problems, additional research should be done to more definitively to determine the Board's role. A different approach to answer the question would involve tracing the Board members' previous assignments to see if they were attached to organizations, like BuOrd, that had additional information that was not presented during Board hearings.

The thesis determined that the SOC acted like a sub-committee to the Board. Additional research that examined SOC transcripts and correspondence could determine how members of the SOC considered their relationship to the Board. The SOC contribution to submarine development was significant and their relationship with the Board should be further explored.

---

[1]Until 1932 the CNO was an ex officio member of the Board and could sit in anytime he wanted at the formal meetings of the executive committee and during the hearings.

Like the SOC, the Bureaus contributed significantly to interwar submarine design and the Board's decisions. The research examined the issue of the relationships between the Board and the Bureaus. Further examination of the relationship in both the studies of the Board resident at the National Archives in Washington DC as well as the archival correspondence and records of the various Bureaus would lead to a better understanding of the Board and Bureaus contributions to submarine design.

Final Thoughts

The Board made significant contributions to submarine design in the interwar period, a period with limited resources. While it would seem to follow that a reduction in money to build submarines and treaty limitations would cause the Board to be less innovative, the opposite was often true. Limited fiscal resources and treaty constraints forced the Board to develop innovative and unique solutions to continue the advancement of submarine design. The Board had a positive impact on most submarine characteristic and specifically the areas examined by the thesis.

GLOSSARY

Diesel electric. Having an electric motor powered directly by an electric generator or by batteries charged by the generator, with the generator being driven by a diesel engine

Interwar. The period following WW I and prior to the start of WW II. (11 November 1918 to 7 December 1941)

Knots. A unit of speed equal to one nautical mile or about 1.15 statute miles per hour.

Nautical Mile. A unit of length used in sea and air navigation, based on the length of one minute of arc of a great circle, especially an international and U.S. unit equal to 1,852 meters (about 6,076 feet). 800 feet longer than a statute mile.

U-boat. A submarine of the German navy.

Submarine. A vessel that can be submerged and navigated under water.

APPENDIX A

INTERWAR U.S. SUBMARINES

The following list of selected submarine data was taken from Friedman's *U.S. Submarines Through 1945* and the Naval Historical Society *Dictionary of American Naval Fighting Ships*. Surfaced displacement was listed without considering extra fuel in ballast tanks.

Submarine	Date Initially Commissioned	Surface Displacement (tons)	Surface Speed (kts)	Surface Endurance (nm/kt)	Torpedo Tubes	Guns	Test Depth (ft)
K-1	17 Mar 1914	392	14	3,150/11	4 bow	--	200
L-1	11 Apr 1916	450	14	3,150/11	4 bow	1x3 in	200
N-1	26 Sep 1917	347	13	3,500/11	4 bow	--	200
O-1	5 Nov 1918	520	14	3,500/11*	4 bow	1x3 in	200
R-1	16 Dec 1918	574	12.5	4,700/6.2	4 bow	1x3 in	200
S-1	5 Jun 1920	854	14.5	5,000/11*	4 bow	1x4 in	200
T-1	3 Jan 1920	1,106	20	3,000/11	4 bow/2 deck	1x4 in	200
V-1 (*Barracuda*)	1 Oct 1924	2,119	21	6,000/11	4 bow/2 stern	1x5 in	200
V-4 (*Argonaut*)	2 Apr 1928	3,046	15	8,000/10	4 bow/2 mine	2x6 in	300
V-5 (*Narwhal*)	15 May 1930	2,730	17	9,380/10	4 bow/2 stern	2x6 in	300
V-7 (*Dolphin*)	1 Jun 1932	1,718	17	4,900/10	4 bow/2 stern	1x4 in	300
V-8 (*Cachalot*)	1 Dec 1933	1,110	17	6,000/10	4 bow/2 stern	1x3 in	250
Porpoise	15 Aug 1935	1,310	19	6,000/10	4 bow/2 stern	1x3 in	250
Shark	25 Jan 1936	1,316	19.5	6,000/10	4 bow/2 stern	1x3 in	250
Perch	19 Nov 1936	1,350	19.25	11,000/10	4 bow/2 stern	1x3 in	250
Salmon	15 Mar 1938	1,435	21	11,000/10	4 bow/4 stern	1x3 in	250
Sargo	7 Feb 1939	1,450	21	11,000/10	4 bow/4 stern	1x3 in	250
Tambor	3 Jun 1940	1,475	20.4	11,000/10	6 bow/4 stern	1x3 in	250
Marlin	1 Aug 1941	800	14.5	7,400/10	4 bow/2 stern	1x3 in	250
Gato	31 Dec 1941	1,526	21	11,000/10	6 bow/4 stern	1x3 in	300
Balao	4 Feb 1943	1,525	20.25	11,000/10	6 bow/4 stern	1x5 in	400

* Not listed by Friedman or Dictionary of American Naval Fighting Ships. Values listed were approximate.

A list of all U.S. submarines made immediately prior to WW I through the USS *Balao.*

(SS-32) K-1
(SS-33) K-2
(SS-34) K-3
(SS-35) K-4
(SS-36) K-5
(SS-37) K-6
(SS-38) K-7
(SS-39) K-8
(SS-40) L-1
(SS-41) L-2
(SS-42) L-3
(SS-43) L-4
(SS-44) L-5
(SS-45) L-6
(SS-46) L-7
(SS-47) M-1
(SS-48) L-8
(SS-49) L-9
(SS-50) L-10
(SS-51) L-11
(SS-52) AA-1/T-1
(SS-53) N-1
(SS-54) N-2
(SS-55) N-3
(SS-56) N-4
(SS-57) N-5
(SS-58) N-6
(SS-59) N-7
(SS-60) AA-2/T-2
(SS-61) AA-3/T-3
(SS-62) O-1
(SS-63) O-2
(SS-64) O-3
(SS-65) O-4
(SS-66) O-5
(SS-67) O-6
(SS-68) O-7
(SS-69) O-8
(SS-70) O-9
(SS-71) O-10
(SS-72) O-11
(SS-73) O-12
(SS-74) O-13
(SS-75) O-14
(SS-76) O-15
(SS-77) O-16
(SS-78) R-1
(SS-79) R-2
(SS-80) R-3
(SS-81) R-4
(SS-82) R-5
(SS-83) R-6
(SS-84) R-7
(SS-85) R-8
(SS-86) R-9
(SS-87) R-10
(SS-88) R-11
(SS-89) R-12
(SS-90) R-13
(SS-91) R-14
(SS-92) R-15
(SS-93) R-16
(SS-94) R-17
(SS-95) R-18
(SS-96) R-19
(SS-97) R-20
(SS-98) R-21
(SS-99) R-22
(SS-100) R-23
(SS-101) R-24
(SS-102) R-25
(SS-103) R-26
(SS-104) R-27
(SS-105) S-1
(SS-106) S-2
(SS-107) S-3
SS-108 cancelled
(SS-109) S-4
(SS-110) S-5
(SS-111) S-6
(SS-112) S-7
(SS-113) S-8
(SS-114) S-9
(SS-115) S-10
(SS-116) S-11
(SS-117) S-12
(SS-118) S-13
(SS-119) S-14
(SS-120) S-15
(SS-121) S-16
(SS-122) S-17
(SS-123) S-18
(SS-124) S-19
(SS-125) S-20
(SS-126) S-21
(SS-127) S-22
(SS-128) S-23
(SS-129) S-24
(SS-130) S-25
(SS-131) S-26
(SS-132) S-27
(SS-133) S-28
(SS-134) S-29
(SS-135) S-30
(SS-136) S-31
(SS-137) S-32
(SS-138) S-33
(SS-139) S-34
(SS-140) S-35
(SS-141) S-36
(SS-142) S-37
(SS-143) S-38
(SS-144) S-39
(SS-145) S-40
(SS-146) S-41
(SS-147) H-4
(SS-148) H-5
(SS-149) H-6
(SS-150) H-7
(SS-151) H-8
(SS-152) H-9
(SS-153) S-42
(SS-154) S-43
(SS-155) S-44
(SS-156) S-45
(SS-157) S-46
(SS-158) S-47
(SS-159) S-48
(SS-160) S-49
(SS-161) S-50
(SS-162) S-51
(SS-163) Barracuda
(SS-164) Bass
(SS-165) Bonita
(SS-166) Argonaut
(SS-167) Narwhal
(SS-168) Nautilus
(SS-169) Dolphin
(SS-170) Cachalot
(SS-171) Cuttlefish
(SS-172) Porpoise
(SS-173) Pike
(SS-174) Shark
(SS-175) Tarpon
(SS-176) Perch
(SS-177) Pickerel
(SS-178) Permit
(SS-179) Plunger
(SS-180) Pollack
(SS-181) Pompano
(SS-182) Salmon
(SS-183) Seal
(SS-184) Skipjack
(SS-185) Snapper
(SS-186) Stingray
(SS-187) Sturgeon
(SS-188) Sargo
(SS-189) Saury
(SS-190) Spearfish
(SS-191) Sculpin
(SS-192) Squalus
(SS-193) Swordfish
(SS-194) Seadragon
(SS-195) Sealion

(SS-196) Searaven
(SS-197) Seawolf
(SS-198) Tambor
(SS-199) Tautog
(SS-200) Thresher
(SS-201) Triton
(SS-202) Trout
(SS-203) Tuna
(SS-204) Mackerel
(SS-205) Marlin
(SS-206) Gar
(SS-207) Grampus
(SS-208) Grayback
(SS-209) Grayling
(SS-210) Grenadier
(SS-211) Gudgeon
(SS-212) Gato
(SS-213) Greenling
(SS-214) Grouper
(SS-215) Growler
(SS-216) Grunion
(SS-217) Guardfish
(SS-218) Albacore
(SS-219) Amberjack
(SS-220) Barb
(SS-221) Blackfish
(SS-222) Bluefish
(SS-223) Bonefish
(SS-224) Cod
(SS-225) Cero
(SS-226) Corvina
(SS-227) Darter
(SS-228) Drum
(SS-229) Flying Fish
(SS-230) Finback
(SS-231) Haddock
(SS-232) Halibut
(SS-233) Herring
(SS-234) Kingfish
(SS-235) Shad
(SS-236) Silversides
(SS-237) Trigger
(SS-238) Wahoo
(SS-239) Whale
(SS-240) Angler
(SS-241) Bashaw
(SS-242) Bluegill
(SS-243) Bream
(SS-244) Cavalla
(SS-245) Cobia
(SS-246) Croaker
(SS-247) Dace
(SS-248) Dorado
(SS-249) Flasher
(SS-250) Flier
(SS-251) Flounder
(SS-252) Gabilan
(SS-253) Gunnel
(SS-254) Gurnard
(SS-255) Haddo
(SS-256) Hake
(SS-257) Harder
(SS-258) Hoe
(SS-259) Jack
(SS-260) Lapon
(SS-261) Mingo
(SS-262) Muskallunge
(SS-263) Paddle
(SS-264) Pargo
(SS-265) Peto
(SS-266) Pogy
(SS-267) Pompon
(SS-268) Puffer
(SS-269) Rasher
(SS-270) Raton
(SS-271) Ray
(SS-272) Redfin
(SS-273) Robalo
(SS-274) Rock
(SS-275) Runner
(SS-276) Sawfish
(SS-277) Scamp
(SS-278) Scorpion
(SS-279) Snook
(SS-280) Steelhead
(SS-281) Sunfish
(SS-282) Tunny
(SS-283) Tinosa
(SS-284) Tullibee
(SS-285) Balao

APPENDIX B

SUBMARINE HEARINGS BEFORE THE BOARD

Year	Starting Page Numbers in Transcripts	Hearing topic
1917	69, 105, 129, 141, 176, 343, 369	General submarine matters; state of U.S. submarine force
1917	306, 390	Submarine detection
1917	455, 686	Offensive war against submarines
1917	533	Chilean submarines
1917	582, 597	Sound detection
1917	617, 633, 645	Air Purification
1917	738, 750	British submarines
1918	83, 131	Listening devices
1918	128	Warfare against submarines
1918	356, 479, 539	General submarine discussion
1918	472	Submarine offensive Dunkirk-Calais
1918	588	Destroyer operations against submarines
1918	964	Armament
1918	1356	Power plants for large submarines
1918	1389	Developments in submarine design
1919	59, 82, 101, 139	Fleet Submarines
1920	133, 164	Fleet Submarines
1920	932, 1014	Propelling Machinery
1921	304, 356	Yates Stirling letter to the Board
1921	386	Neff propulsion system
1922	397	Neff propulsion system
1922	721	Scout and mine laying submarines
1923	80	Cruiser and mine laying submarines
1924	273, 323	Cruiser and mine laying submarines
1924	350	V-4
1925	259, 492	Cruiser submarines
1926	237	Long range submarines
1926	313	S-class submarines; V-7, V-8 and V-9
1927	67, 135	1929 building program
1928	129	Submarine characteristics
1928	357	Future submarines
1929	128, 185	V-7, V-8 and V-9
1929	152	Discussions with Electric Boat
1929	369	V-1 through V-3 overweight condition
1930	74, 107	V-7, V-8 and V-9
1930	253	Main engines and auxiliaries for V-8 and V-9
1930	267, 363, 401, 421	Future submarines
1933	64	Submarine characteristics
1935	29, 60	Submarine 182-187
1936	8	Submarine characteristics of the 1938 building program
1937	94, 320	Submarine characteristics of the 1939 building program
1938	49	Submarine characteristics of the 1940 building program
1939	348	Submarine characteristics of the 1941 building program
1940	269	Submarine characteristics of the 1942 building program
1940	445	Submarine carrying aviation gasoline

BIBLIOGRAPHY

Archival Sources

Combined Arms Research Library, Fort Leavenworth, KS Archival Information Proceedings and Hearings of the General Board of the U.S. Navy, 1900-1950 (Microfilm).

Guide to the Scholarly Resources Microfilm Edition of the Hearings before the General Board of the Navy, 1917-50. Lists specific topics and provides the year, volume, page number, and microfilm roll number for that topic., Wilmington, DE: Scholarly Resources, 1983.

Naval Historical Center. *Dictionary of American Naval Fighting Ships, Volumes I - VIII.* Edited by James L. Mooney. Washington, DC: U.S. Government Printing Office, 1991.

Published Primary Sources, Articles, and Memoirs

Galantin, Ignatius. *Submarine Admiral: From Battlewagons to Ballistic Missiles.* Urbana: University of Illinois Press, 1995.

Lockwood, Charles. *Down to the Sea in Subs.* New York: W. W. Norton & Co., 1967.

———. *Sink 'Em All.* New York: Bantam Books, 1951.

O'Kane, Richard. *Clear the Bridge.* Novato, CA: Presidio Press, 1977.

Stirling, Yates. *Sea Duty: The Memoirs of a Fighting Admiral.* New York: G.P. Putnam's Sons, 1939.

Books

Alden, John D. *The Fleet Submarine in the U. S. Navy.* Annapolis, MD: Naval Institute Press, 1979.

Bagnasco, Erminio. *Submarines of World War Two.* Annapolis: Naval Institute Press, 1977.

Blair, Clay, Jr. *Silent Victory*. Philadelphia: Lippincott, 1975.

Bowen, Harold G. *Ships, Machinery, and Mossbacks.* Princeton, NJ: University Press, 1954.

Friedman, Norman. *Submarine Design and Development.* London: Conway Maritime Press, 1984.

Hackmann, Willem D. *Seek and Strike: Sonar, Anti-Submarine Warfare and the Royal Navy 1914-54.* London: Stationery Office Books, 1984.

Halpern, Paul G. *A Naval History of World War I.* Annapolis: Naval Institute Press, 1994.

Harris, Brayton. *Submarines: A Political, Social And Military History.* New York: Berkley Books, 1997.

Hooks, Gregory. *Forging the Military-Industrial Complex.* Urbana: University of Illinois Press, 1991.

Hoyt, Edwin P. *Submarines at War: The History of the Silient Service.* New York: Stein and Day, 1983.

Kuehn, John T. *Agents of Innovation: The General Board and the Design of the Fleet that Defeated the Japanese* . Annapolis, MD: Naval Institute Press, 2008.

Leutze, James. *A Different Kind of Victory: A Biography of Admiral Thomas C. Hark.* Annapolis: Naval Institute Press, 1981.

Miller, Edward S. *War Plan Orange.* Annapolis: Naval Institute Press, 1991.

Murray, Williamson, and Allan Millett. *Military Innovation in the Interwar Period.* Cambridge: Cambridge University Press, 1996.

Polmar, Norman. *The American Submarine.* Annapolis: The Nautical and Aviation Publishing Company of America, 1981.

Roskill, Stephen. *Naval Policy between the Wars, Vol 1: The Period of Anglo-American Antagonism, 1919-1929.* London: Collins, 1968.

Sims, William S. *The Victory at Sea.* Annapolis: U.S. Naval Institute Press , 1984.

Turabian, Kate L. *A Manual for Writers.* 6th ed. Revised by. John Grossman and Alice Bennett. Chicago: University of Chicago Press, 1996.

Weir, Gary. *Building American Submarines 1914-1940.* Washington DC: Naval Historical Center, 1991.

Theses and Dissertations

Kuehn, John T. "The Influence of Naval Arms Limitation on U.S. Naval Innovation During the Interwar Period, 1921-1937." Ph.D. Dissertation, Kansas State University, Manhattan, 2007.

Articles and Lectures

Andrade, Ernest. “Submarine Policy in the United States Navy, 1919-1941.” *Military Affairs* (1971): 50-56.

Shireman, Douglas A. "U.S. Torpedo Troubles During World War II." *World War II Magazine* (February 1998). http://www.historynet.com/us-torpedo-troubles-during-world-war-ii.htm/ (accessed February 22, 2009).

Whitman, Edward C. "The Navy’s Variegated V-Class." *Undersea Warfare* (Fall 2008). http://www.navy.mil/navydata/cno/n87/usw/issue_20vclass.htm (accessed December 18, 2008).

———. "The School of War: U.S. Submarines in World War I." *Undersea Warfare* (Spring 2004). http://www.navy.mil/navydata/cno/n87/usw/issue_22/ ww1.htm (accessed September 7, 2008).

INITIAL DISTRIBUTION LIST

Combined Arms Research Library
U.S. Army Command and General Staff College
250 Gibbon Ave.
Fort Leavenworth, KS 66027-2314

Defense Technical Information Center/OCA
825 John J. Kingman Rd., Suite 944
Fort Belvoir, VA 22060-6218

Naval History and Heritage Command
Department of the Navy -- Naval Historical Center
805 Kidder Breese SE -- Washington Navy Yard
Washington DC, 20374-5060

Naval War College
686 Cushing Road
Newport, RI 02841-1207

U.S. Naval Academy
History Department
107 Maryland Avenue
Annapolis, MD 21402

Naval Postgraduate School
Department of History
1 University Circle
Monterey, CA 93943

Dr. John T. Kuehn
DMH, USACGSC
100 Stimson Ave.
Fort Leavenworth, KS 66027-2301

Mr. Harold A. Laurence
DJIMO, USACGSC
100 Stimson Ave.
Fort Leavenworth, KS 66027-2301

Mr. Bob A. King
DJIMO, USACGSC
100 Stimson Ave.
Fort Leavenworth, KS 66027-2301

www.ingramcontent.com/pod-product-compliance
Lightning Source LLC
LaVergne TN
LVHW061246100826
845148LV00008B/1036
* 9 7 8 1 6 0 8 8 8 2 6 8 7 *